A RACE OF EXTREMES: 25 EXCEPTIONAL FORMULA 1 STORIES

ABOUT WHAT HAPPENED ON AND OFF THE TRACK

ROY LINGSTER

CONTENTS

INTRODUCTION

> "*There are only three sports: bullfighting, motor racing, and mountaineering; all the rest are merely games.*"[1]
>
> — ERNEST HEMINGWAY

There is a strong possibility that, as a driver, you have had at least one exhilarating moment behind the wheel. Maybe it was the first time you drove by yourself after getting your license or opening up on the highway in your new car. And what about that rush when you go to overtake, knowing your exit is coming up? Of course, there have probably been some terrifying moments, like an idiot driver or black ice to contend with. Either way, you always need to have your wits about you as you just don't know what is around the corner.

This begs the question, how difficult can it be to drive 190 miles around the same track at least 50 times? Isn't Formula 1 just a case of cars going round and round making a lot of noise? Let's face it: it's not like drivers have to run 5 or 6 miles like a professional football player would. Formula 1 drivers are sitting down, and the hardest thing they have to do is control a car specifically designed to drive at high speeds and varying conditions. They don't even have to change their own tires? Can you even class Formula 1 as a sport, at least with the same passion as Hemingway?

Not only is Formula 1 a sport, it is actually one of the most mentally and physically demanding sports in the world! Even the most avid fan might roll an eye at that statement, but let's take a look at the facts.

It takes a surprising amount of control to keep Formula 1 cars on the track, and this requires strength training, especially in the core and neck muscles so that they can stand the length of a race. Professional races train in a similar manner to Olympic athletes. During a race, a Formula 1 driver has to cope with G-forces up to five times gravity bearing down on them as they drive at average speeds of 136 miles per hour (MPH). Drivers must train their cardiovascular system to ensure their muscles get sufficient oxygen.

On a hot summer's day, your air conditioning does a nice job of keeping you cool. You may even roll a window down and enjoy the breeze! Air conditioning in a Formula 1 car would be completely ineffective as the cockpit can reach temperatures of 122°F. In just one race, drivers can lose nearly 5 percent of their body weight in sweat.

The cardiovascular system has to be even more efficient to combat the effects of the heat combined with the G-Force, which requires similar training to that of a marathon runner.

Rarely do we see the physical demands drivers are under. Add this to the competitiveness and concentration required, and you can soon see that Formula 1 is extremely demanding.

It hasn't always been this way. Today's Formula 1 car has a top speed of around 225 MPH and can do 0 to 60 in just 2 seconds. The Alfa Romeo 158 (also known as the Alfetta) was the winning car of the first Formula 1 in 1950 and had a top speed of 180 MPH; it took twice as long to get from 0 to 60. It's hard to imagine the differences in technology both under the hood and in the cockpit. While modern drivers are under far more pressure than the superstars of the 50s, they are able to drive in the safest conditions ever seen.

All sports undergo change over time, but few have seen the same degree of change as Formula 1. Watching a race today makes it easy to forget the rich history of racing. As a fan, keeping up with your favorite driver and team is important. To be considered a true fan, one who can fascinate friends and family with unknown tales, it's necessary to delve into this history, the changes, and some of the most exceptional moments of Formula 1.

You don't even need to be a Formula 1 fan to enjoy the stories you are about to discover. Twenty-five years ago, I began playing baseball as a hobby. As a military sports instructor, I had always had a passion for sports, but baseball led me to coaching, and this opened the doors to a love of basketball and football. I was happy to try practically any physical activity, but Formula 1 had never been a huge interest to me.

It wasn't until I had a severe setback that allowed me to learn more about the trials and tribulations of racing. One particular story got me hooked and helped me to discover inspiration and resilience. It's amazing how what you can learn from epic stories in any sport can change your life and even open the doors to new opportunities.

As baseball was my first love, it was logical for my first book to be based on this topic. After publishing *The Baseball Player's Guide to Hitting Like a Pro*, I decided to create a series of Books, *A Game of Extremes*, as a way to share epic sporting stories so that more people can experience the same benefits I have had while writing about them. Although there are a number of excellent sporting books on the market, I wanted to take a different approach.

Instead of focusing on sporting events you would hear in the media, my goal is to spread a love for learning about sports as they have evolved over the years and the epic events that have been forgotten. During the research of this book, I was amazed, shocked, saddened, awed, motivated, and everything in between. Whether you are eight or 80, you drive a Ford or a Porche, there will be challenges and obstacles that can set you back. What drives me as a writer (pun intended) is that these Formula 1 stories help you find it in yourself to keep going, handle the pressure, and succeed on the other side.

What better way to begin our stories of extreme races than with one of the sport's legends and only one of four drivers awarded a knighthood by the late Queen of England!

1

THE GREATEST DRIVER NEVER TO WIN FORMULA 1 WORLD CHAMPIONSHIP

"In order to finish first, first you have to finish."[1]

— STIRLING MOSS

It's hard to imagine a driver that competed in 529 races could win 212 of them, participate in and win 16 Grand Prix, but never win a World Championship. If that didn't sting Stirling Moss, the fact that he missed out on that World Championship win by one point must have hurt!

Moss was born in 1929 in London. His mom, Aileen Moss, raced in hill climbs, and his dad, Alfred Moss, was an amateur racing driver. There was little doubt of Moss's future on the track. His dad gave him his first car at the age of nine. He would drive that Austin 7 in the fields around his home. As soon as he got his license at 15, Moss bought a Morris Minor and started entering local races. Fortunately, Moss had a second hobby, horse riding. Thanks to the money he earned from horse-riding events, he could put a deposit down on a Cooper 500.

In 1948, Moss made his debut in Formula 3. Two years later, just before his 21st birthday, he won his first international race, capturing the attention of Ferrari inventor Enzo Ferrari. His rise to fame was fast. In the same year, he moved up to Formula 2 and entered his first Formula 1 race with the exceptional HWM Alta Jaguar. In the Swiss Grand Prix in 1951, Moss came in seventh place, but perhaps more significant was that this was where he first raced against Juan Manuel Fangio, who would go on to be his rival, friend, and mentor.

Aside from his exceptional driving skills, Stirling Moss was known for his incredible loyalty. Though Ferrari attempted to convince Moss to join the team, Moss was not happy when he discovered Ferrari had given the car to another driver. This only reinforced his commitment to British cars. Of the 84 different cars he raced during his career, most were British. Moss once said, "Better to lose honorably in a British car than win in a foreign one. [2]

The titles for Moss kept accumulating. In the early 50s, Moss won a Coupe d'Or, and he became the first non-American to win the 12 Hours of Sebring. Moss's talent was obvious, but his cars hadn't been enough to see a Formula 1 win. That was until Mercedes boss Alfred

Neubauer took Moss's career to the next level. Moss achieved his first Formula 1 win at the British Grand Prix in 1955. It was an incredible race for Moss, beating his teammate Fangio and allowing a 1-2-3-4 win for Mercedes. On top of that, Moss became the first ever British driver to win a British Grand Prix. Although he was convinced Fangio had let him win, Fangio admitted that Moss had been the better driver ... that day.

Still, this was not the race that Moss considered his greatest drive ever. Skip forward to 1961; Mercedes had withdrawn from Formula 1 after the Le Mans disaster when the Mercedes 300 SLR took off and launched into the crowd. This left Moss driving a privately owned aging Lotus 18. Moss had earned pole position, and in any other race, this would have been a relief if it hadn't been for the two modern Ferrari's driven by Richie Ginther and Phil Hill right behind him.

Moss sat at the starting line, knowing he would need a perfect lap to beat the Ferraris, but he also knew that a perfect lap was nearly impossible. Cars were narrower in those days, but curbs were much higher than they are today. The slightest touch of a curb and the Lotus's wheel would have come off.

The race lasted a grueling 2 hours and 46 minutes. Moss initially lost the lead to Ginther and then Jim Clark in another Lotus, but after Clark pulled into the pit, Moss was able to pass. The race was now between the Lotus and the Ferraris, with Moss taking the lead on the 14th lap. Each time Hill or Ginther took the lead, Moss came back. This went on for 100 laps. At one point, both Ferraris were just seconds behind, and Moss thought the drivers were doing it on purpose, waiting until the last lap to speed past him, but that never happened. The Ferrari team was left stunned as Moss and his aged lotus took the flag first!

For Moss, this was his greatest race because of the sheer concentration it took over such a long period of time. But it is races like this that only add to the question: How could such an able, successful driver never become a World Champion? Again, his loyalty and sportsmanship can answer that question.

Prior to his greatest race, Moss competed in the 1958 Portuguese Grand Prix. This was a Grand Prix race like no other, even before the start. Unlike the typical track you would see today, this race was to be held in the streets of Oporto. Curbs, trees, lampposts, shops, and houses were some of the things drivers would have to navigate, but what made Oporto one of the toughest street tracks were the cobbles, made even more challenging that day by the damp, cloudy weather. Then there were the electric train tracks, protected by hay bales! Dangerous tracks were all part of the norm in those days, and nobody even thought of complaining.

Moss, in his Vanwall, had pole position, and in second position with just a 0.05-second difference was Moss's friend Mike Hawthorn in his Ferrari. Despite being friends, the competition was intense. There were just two races left in the season before the champion would gain their title, and the battle was between Moss and Hawthorn. Not only would the winner be the World Champion, but they would also be the first Brit to achieve this title.

Hawthorn took the lead on the second lap, but by the seventh lap, Moss had overtaken. By lap 25, Moss had a clear 1-minute lead due to Hawthorn's pit stop for his brakes. Moss let Hawthorn unlap himself, putting the Ferrari ahead. After an extremely tight corner (between houses and shops), Hawthorn spun and stalled. In an act that would be rare to see today, Moss stopped and watched to make sure his friend was okay. Any outside assistance from officials would have led to disqualification, so Moss and Hawthorn waved them on. Moss went on to win first place and Hawthorn second.

Officials weren't happy because they thought Hawthorn had attempted to restart his car in the opposite direction, against traffic, which would have meant disqualification for breach of rules. Moss came to the defense without hesitation and confirmed Hawthorn wasn't on the track, so officials allowed Hawthorn to keep his six points for second place and the extra point for the fastest lap. Had Moss not come forward, he would have gone on to become the first British World Champion. As it happened, Hawthorn earned the title by one single extra point.

Moss's professional racing career ended abruptly in 1962 after a horrific accident that he was lucky to survive. He was thrown from his Lotus after hitting a bank at high speed. He was in a coma for a month, and it took 6 months for him to recover from being partially paralyzed. This didn't stop him from racing historic cars until he was 81 as well as commenting and writing about the sport. As an ambassador for motorsports and his significant contributions to racing, the Queen knighted him Sir Stirling Moss in 2000.

2

THE TRAGIC END TO WHAT WOULD BECOME LEGENDARY

"Life is measured in achievement not in years alone."[1]

— BRUCE MCLAREN

The British aren't only famous for their incredible drivers, they are also famous for their innovative racing cars. McLaren has become a powerhouse for racing cars and record-setting. For over two decades, McLaren held the record for the fastest speed of 243 miles per hour.[2] The company was also the first to use a carbon fiber monocoque chassis, allowing for more durable, lighter, and stronger cars. Furthermore, they are proactive about becoming an eco-friendly company, committing to reducing CO_2 emissions and recycling 60 percent of the company's waste. It's such a shame that the founder's life was cut short before any of these achievements were seen.

Bruce Leslie McLaren was born in Auckland, New Zealand in 1937. His father owned a garage and raced motorbikes, though he later raced sports cars, too. At school, McLaren was a huge rugby fan and captain of his primary school team. His dreams of contact sports ended too soon when he contracted Legg-Calvé-Perthes disease, a very rare childhood hip disorder. At nine years old, McLaren spent a month in the hospital and two years in a wheelchair before learning how to walk again. He would never lose the limp in his leg; perhaps it was a constant reminder of what he achieved through determination.

He was fascinated by all things related to engineering. He would strip his bike to make it go faster, and by 15, he had taught himself to drive and began racing competitively. In 1956, McLaren went to Auckland University to study engineering, and the following year, he was awarded the first "Driver to Europe" scholarship. This was perfect for McLaren as, at the time, eight of the 11 Formula 1 races were in Europe. Fellow driver Colin Beanland went with McLaren as his mechanic.

McLaren entered his first Formula 2 race in a car that he and Beanland had assembled themselves and was soon asked to join the Cooper Formula 1 team. He won his first Grand Prix in the U.S. in 1959. At only 22 years old he became the youngest driver to win an international Grand Prix, a record that wouldn't be beaten until 2003! He also went on to win the 1960 Argentina Grand Prix, the 1962 Monaco Grand Prix, and the 1968 Belgium Grand Prix.

In between all of this, McLaren still found time to begin his own racing car company. In 1963, Bruce McLaren Motor Racing Ltd was formed, and McLaren's leadership style spurred enthusiasm across the entire team. Not only did McLaren design and drive the cars, but he would also transport vehicles and sweep the factory floor if needed.

McLaren's first successful car was the McLaren M6A, which was designed in 11 weeks. The nose, raised tail, and wedge-like shape made the car stand out on the track, but business partner Teddy Mayer thought the unique papaya orange paint would stand out more on black and white television screens. McLaren and the M6A won the 1976 Can-Am Challenge Cup.

In 1966, one of McLaren's cars first entered a Formula 1 race, and two years later, McLaren won a Grand Prix with his M7C. This car went down in history as the most successful engine in F1 history. It scored points in every race it finished!

McLaren's ambition was unlimited. In 1969, McLaren manufactured the M6GT, the first-ever road car that he used to get to work. His dream was to create the fastest accelerating road car. The plan was for the company to produce 250 M6GTs, and at the beginning of the 1970 season, McLaren admitted to friends that it would be his last year racing to focus on his latest ambition. In the end, only four M6GTs were made: two in red, one in yellow, and the fourth in the famous McLaren orange. The value of this car today is estimated at $1,500,000!

The reason why the company didn't reach its target with the M6GT is tragic. In 1970, the team decided it would go for another record, entering the Grand Prix series, the Can-Am, and the Indy 500 race. In June 1970, McLaren was in Goodwood testing the M8D after its predecessor, the M8B, had won all of the races entered in 1960. The M8D, commonly known as the "Batmobile," had already been tested several times, but on the final test run, going at 169 MPH, the rear fairing and wing broke off, leaving the car with no downforce. The car hit a marshal's post, and McLaren was killed instantly.

Considering what an inspirational leader McLaren had been, the team took the news of his passing hard. Teddy Mayer, who went on to lead the team, broke the news on the workshop floor, encouraging the shattered members to go home and take some time to themselves. Despite the devastation, nobody could keep away, and the following day, team members all found their way to the workshop that would never be the same again. Mayer addressed the team:

> "Well, we don't have a boss, we don't have a driver, and we don't even have a car. But we do have a motor race- at Mosport in two week's time- and we all owe it to Bruce to race. So we might as well get to it."[3]

Not only did they race, but the team won—a sure sign that McLaren's determination and ambition would live on in all his team members. The McLaren M8D went on to win all races in the season except one. McLaren has the longest history in Formula 1 history, except for Ferrari, and his dream of making road cars was achieved. Of all the road models McLaren has built, the F1 is still considered one of the greatest supercars ever built. With only 106 F1 cars produced, it is one of the fastest cars of its time, engineered to perfection, and in true McLaren style, a record breaker on so many levels.

3

THE FIRST GRAND PRIX TO LIGHT UP THE NIGHT SKY

> " *I think it is a big, big step forward for Formula One. The pictures, the atmosphere is really one of a kind and this gives a completely new experience to all the viewers worldwide but also to the spectators.*"[1]
>
> — NORBERT HAUG

The Singapore Grand Prix is associated with luxury and parties, with a Platinum VIP package going for S$25,000.[2] At least the 30 guests get 6 bottles of champagne, 2 bottles of Belvedere Vodka, and a bottle of Johnnie Walker Blue Label (among other treats). While you can expect glitz and glam, you wouldn't expect the first-ever nighttime Grand Prix to be so controversial.

Rarely is there a Grand Prix race that doesn't have some drama, but in 2008, the Singapore Grand Prix saw the beginnings of a drama that would unfold 15 years later. The atmosphere around the track was incredible. The 3.1-mile circuit had been designed to test drivers to their limits. There were a record-breaking 300,000 attendees as 1,500 projected lights lit the dark sky. The audience was on the edges of their seats, waiting to see what would happen in the next stage of the McLaren and Ferrari toxic rivalry.

Felipe Massa for Ferrari had gained pole position, with Lewis Hamilton for McLaren-Mercedes in second position. Teammates Fernando Alonso and Nelson Piquet Jr. for Renault had both had a frustrating season, and the qualifiers left them in 15th and 16th position. Both drivers struggled to move from these positions at the beginning of the race while Massa zoomed ahead in the lead.

On lap 14, Piquet Jr. crashed. He claimed there had been a lot of graining (too much heat on the surface of tires, which causes tire strips to tear away) at the start of the race, leading to him losing the rear of the car. What happened next changed the course of the entire race.

Under the 2008 rules, the pit lanes were closed any time a safety car was deployed. Drivers needing to stop had a 10-second stop-and-go penalty. Not wanting a penalty, many drivers waited until Piquet Jr.'s car had been removed before stopping, and others had to suffer the penalty. This meant that after the leading cars refueled and served their penalty time, Alonso was suddenly in the lead.

The pit stops were more painful for Massa as he drove off with the fuel rig stuck in his Ferrari. He stopped at the end of the pit lane, but not before taking out one of his own mechanics! Unfortunately, what seemed like an inevitable win for Ferrari ended up with Massa coming in 13th. Alonso was first to see the checkered flag, Nico Rosberg stole second place, and Lewis Hamilton reached third. This enabled Hamilton to become the 2008 champion, with Massa missing out by just one point.

One accident can change the outcome for many. One could say it's simply a part of the sport. What should never be part of any sport is a conspiracy, and this is what came to light 15 years later!

In the 2008 race, Renault's leaders had told Piquet Jr. to crash strategically after Alonso stopped for new tires. They knew the 2008 pit stop regulations and knew the safety car would be deployed. When Piquet's father found out, he contacted Bernie Ecclestone, the then-chief of the Formula One Group. He discussed the situation with the FIA president, Max Mosely. Between them, they decided that sharing the information would create a scandal that they wanted to protect racing from. It was in the best interest of Formula 1, especially as the rules stated that once a champion had been decided and had received the trophy, nothing could be changed.

The injustices kept coming. The relationship between Piquet Jr. and Renault broke down when Renault sacked and threatened to take Piquet Jr. to court. It wasn't until transcripts between Piquet Jr. and Renault leaders Flavio Briatore and Pat Symonds emerged that the truth was finally revealed.[3] Briatore was banned from Formula 1 for life, and Symonds received a five-year ban. Piquet Jr. was given immunity because he came forward, though his career as a Formula 1 driver ended. Alonso claimed he knew nothing about the conspiracy.

None of that would help Massa. At the time, Ferrari's lawyers and other lawyers said nothing could be done. But if officials had canceled that race, Hamilton wouldn't have won his first of seven world championships.

Through legal action, Massa hopes to gain more clarity on what happened during the 2008 Singapore Grand Prix. Although championships have been overturned in other sports, such as in the case of Lance Armstrong and the International Cycling Union, for Massa, this might be more difficult. Mosley passed away in 2021, and Ecclestone is 91.

If he is successful, Formula 1 could see more victims of similar situations coming out of the woodwork. On the other hand, if nothing changes, Formula 1 will have this colossal injustice hanging over its history. Perhaps the biggest injustice is that while Massa still doesn't have his title, both Briatore and Symonds have since returned to Formula 1.

4

THE MCLAREN RIVALRY THE WORLD LOVED TO WATCH

"Being second is to be the first of the ones to lose."[1]

— AYRTON SENNA

There are rivalries in all sports. Participating and watching wouldn't be the same without this heated competition. However, most rivalries are between countries or teams within a country. The competition heats up when the two competitors are on the same team, which was the case for McLaren-Honda. The racing world was captivated as this rivalry went on not just for a few races but for two whole seasons.

Ayrton Senna was born in Brazil in 1960. His family was wealthy, and racing was a passion rather than a need for income. His love began at the age of four when his dad bought him a miniature go-kart. At 13, he was racing karts and saw immediate success. Eight years later, he was racing single-seaters for Britain. His driving style was aggressive, fearless, highly skillful, and incredibly brave.

Alain Prost was born in France 5 years earlier. Unlike Senna, Prost's family wasn't as wealthy, and after leaving school, Prost supported his kart racing career by tuning engines. He saw his first professional success in 1978 and then again in 1978, winning both the French and European championships in Formula 3. On the contrary to Senna's aggression and risk, Prost was more calculated, precise, and relied on strategies. This often led him to be nicknamed "The Professor."

The first race between the legends took place in none other than the narrow streets of Monaco in 1984. Senna was racing for Toleman, a small team using the previous year's car. Many imagined that this car was no match for the McLarens (raced by Prost and Niki Lauda). By the 14th lap, Senna had made it from starting in 13th position to 3rd place with just the two McLarens ahead. Senna performed one of the most amazing overtakes, considering the wet conditions. With Senna just 7 seconds away from Prost, the race was suspended because it became too dangerous, sealing a win for Prost and second place for Senna. And so the rivalry began.

From here, Senna went on to race with Lotus before joining McLaren in 1988. Senna vowed to challenge Prost, and this was the year the rivalry started to get interesting.

From 1984 to 1986, Prost had more wins in all three seasons and was named champion in the 1985 and 1986 seasons. The year before Senna joined McLaren, Senna had picked up more wins. The French Grand Prix was when Prost gave Senna's confidence a decent shake. Prost took pole position, something that had been Senna's for the whole season. Despite Senna getting ahead after pitstops, a momentary lapse in concentration enabled Prost to shoot ahead and win the race. Just a few weeks later, the two appeared in an interview. Prost asked if it was possible to be equal, and Senna replied with an awkward laugh and a firm no. The end of the season resulted in Prost with 308 points and Senna with 277. However, because of the points system of the time, only the 11 best races counted toward the championship, and Senna won.

Things turned less friendly in Imola 1989 with the San Marino Grand Prix. The two had a gentleman's agreement not to challenge one another when they reached the first corner. Senna got the better initial start, but after a crash, Prost got off to a better restart. Their agreement was soon forgotten by Senna, who assumed it didn't hold up after the crash. As he screeched around the corner, taking the lead, Prost was left livid, and the tension was still noticed on the podium.

This was also the year that racing fans saw one of Prost and Senna's most notorious crashes. During the Japanese Grand Prix, the two collided at the last chicane. Prost retired immediately, but Senna decided to push start his car and go on to win the race. Soon after, Senna was disqualified, and Prost was announced the winner, which also helped him achieve the season championship, making the tension a little more bitter. This would be Prost's last season with McLaren despite having two years left on his contract. His decision to move to Ferrari had nothing to do with the very public rivalry between the McLaren drivers.

Although Prost was now driving for Ferrari, it didn't stop history from repeating itself in the 1990 Japanese Grand Prix. Senna had a pole position but wasn't happy about starting on the dirtier side of the track. Once again, issues came up with the first corner. Senna had promised no backing down if Prost outpaced him into the first corner. The Ferrari did exactly that, pushing Senna's aggressive style to a jaw-dropping collision. Once again, Senna claimed the championship that season.

Things didn't ease up in the following season, either. In the German Grand Prix, Prost was driving his Ferrari (which he had compared to a horrible truck) with eight laps left to pass Senna and secure 3rd place. As the rivals went into a chicane, Senna subtly opened his steering in the braking zone enough to frighten Prost and for his car to run off and stall.

Even though Senna's aggression seemed to cause the most problems on the track, it was still Senna who did more of the public shaming. News of Prost's intended move to Williams only encouraged Senna to say that Prost was behaving like a coward at a press conference during the 1992 Portuguese Grand Prix.

Nearly 10 years after their first race together, the rivalry between the two drivers seemed to disperse as quickly as their champagne on the podiums. Prost was retiring, and Adelaide was their last race together. It felt like their racing history had completed its circle, with Prost winning Senna's first race and Senna winning Prost's final. On the podium, you could see that the tension had lifted, with Prost even pulling Senna onto the top podium with him more than once.

Prost was obviously determined to be the best driver he could but never had the same fierce motivation to beat Senna as Senna had to beat Frost. Prost has always had great relationships with his teammates. That last day on the podium was the moment that Senna no longer saw Prost as his rival, and although it was Prost's retirement, Senna lost something more than his rival that day.

Prost always believed Senna was lost after retirement; "I felt he was not well."[2] During one race in Imola, Senna actually radioed from the cockpit with a special message saying how much his friend Alain was missed. Although they had never phoned each other while racing together, Senna would call Prost often after his retirement.

One of the sport's sourest rivalries took a complete 360-degree turn once Senna had lost his source of motivation, and, in its place, grew one of the most unlikely friendships. Just a year later, Prost was a pallbearer at Senna's funeral!

5

WHEN TIRES LEAVE A RACE A DRIVER OR TWO SHORT

> " *"This was a sad day for the race fans and it was also a sad to see the other cars pull into the pits, but I guess their problem must have been a serios one."*[1]

— RUBENS BARRICHELLO

The technology in a Formula 1 car is exceptional. Between the controls, instrumentation, and monitoring, there can be 250 individual sensors. It goes without saying that technology has made a significant impact on the performance of these cars, but you can't forget the importance of tires. When a set of tires doesn't work precisely as a diver would like, it's difficult to get the best possible performance out of a racing car, regardless of the technology. At the end of the day, they're the only part of the car in contact with the track and can literally make or break a driver's chance of success.

Over the history of Formula 1, tires have been supplied by the likes of Goodyear, Firestone, Bridgestone, and Dunlop, to name a few. Of the 10 tire suppliers, Pirelli has the greatest history and has played a crucial role in the development of tires. In 2007, FIA introduced a new rule where all cars would be supplied with the same tires. This would prevent any unfair advantages and ensure maximum safety. Since 2011, Pirelli has been the supplier for all Formula 1, 2, and 3 cars.

Each car has three sets of specially constructed tires of different compounds: soft, medium, and hard. Soft tires have the best grip but are the least durable, whereas hard tires are more durable but don't provide the same grip. Medium tires have the optimal balance of the two qualities, but the rules state that drivers must use at least two tire compounds in each race. If the weather is wet, drivers can choose between full-wet tires or a single set of intermediate tires.

As of 2023, teams are allocated eight sets of soft tires, three sets of medium tires, two sets of hard tires, four sets of intermediate tires, and three sets of full wet tires.[2] During each practice race, two sets of tires must be returned, so teams will have seven sets of tires for the qualifiers and the race. Before a Grand Prix race, around 2,300 tires arrive at the location.

In 2005, before the rule of only one supplier was introduced, drivers faced another rule change. Drivers were only allowed a single set of tires for both qualifying and the race. Bridgestone had been supplying Ferrari, Jordan, and Minardi, and Michelin provided the tires for McLaren, Renault, Williams, and Toyota. One provider would have massive difficulties with the Indianapolis Motor Speedway!

It all began on an average Friday morning with drivers testing the track. Ricardo Zonta spun his Toyota, and his left rear Michelin tire went down. Ralf Schumacher crashed on the 13th turn also due to the left rear tire failing. Turn 13 was causing problems because the famous curve was putting abnormal amounts of pressure on the tires. Michelin ordered a new set of tires, but they, too, were failing. After several teams using Michelin noticed the same issue, it was suggested to Bernie Ecclestone and Tony George (Indy boss) that a chicane should be put in before the turn so that cars would slow down. Teams left the track on Saturday, assuming a chicane would be added.

However, adding a chicane so late in the game was impossible for safety reasons and because it would be unfair to other teams. Sunday morning began with several heated meetings. Michelin was still arguing for a chicane, but FIA came back with the option to lift the ban on one set of tires for the whole race. Other ideas included running cars through the pitlane each lap and setting a speed limit for cars using Michelin tires. None of these options appealed to drivers.

As the meeting continued, it became clear that the chicane was necessary, as Michelin teams told officials that they wouldn't be able to race if changes to the track weren't made. Charlie Whiting (FIA race director) was dragged into the meeting and, upon hearing tires were being moved from the 10th turn for the chicane, he immediately announced that if the chicane were built, there would be no race. FIA wouldn't accept it as a FIA race; therefore, it wouldn't be counted toward the World Championship.

According to contracts, all cars had to appear on the grid, so all 20 cars made it to the grid and performed the formation lap. In the most bizarre scene, 14 cars with Michelin tires withdrew to the pits, leaving only cars with Bridgestone tires starting the race: two from Ferrari, two from Toyota, and two from Minardi.

Michael Schumacher came in first, followed by teammate Rubens Barrichello, which was fortunate for Ferrari; it was Schumacher and Ferrari's only win of the season. However, that will always be overshadowed by the disastrous lead-up to the race and the fallout afterward.

Michelin had agreed to subsidize tickets at the 2006 event. Teams using Michelin had to attend a World Sport Motor Council Hearing. They were found guilty of failing to ensure they had suitable tires and of wrongfully refusing to start a race, knowing they had the right to use the pitlane.[3] It was complicated and messy as lawyers said if the drivers had raced knowing there was a defect with the tires, they could have been responsible for criminal negligence under Indiana law, as technically, they were putting the marshals' lives in danger.

Fortunately, Michelin took more than the necessary steps to right the wrong, and they were able to compete in 2006, their final year before withdrawing from Formula 1.

6

EVERY MILLISECOND COUNTS

> *"F1 teams need a driver who will consistently set lap times that are 100 percent on the edge."*[1]
>
> — JEAN ALESI

Motor racing didn't begin with Formula 1, and despite the rich British history, the first Grand Prix took place in France—Le Mans in 1906 with a whopping 32 cars. Before that, motor racing began to take place as far back as 1884, again in France. There was no timing of laps. The winner was simply the first car to reach one village from another. Today, cars are fitted with a transponder that tracks time to within a ten-thousandth of a second.

Each track is fitted with timing loops. These are wires that run across the track every 150 to 200 meters.

Transponders on the car and these timing loops communicate with each other via radio waves. Each car's transponder transmits a unique code through individual radio frequencies, so there is no interference. This system allows for accuracy when monitoring the timings of each car. Thanks to the ever-improving technology, we are able to explore some of Formula 1's closest finishes.[2]

One of the most exciting races of the 60s was seen in the Italian Gran Prix in 1967. Jim Clark kept fans on their toes. After Clark's Lotus experienced a puncture, he managed to regain the lead position with eight laps to go, an incredible comeback alone. But John Surtees and Jack Brabham sped past after the Lotus slowed down because of a faulty fuel pump. Surtees beat Braham over the line by just 0.2 seconds.

In 2002, Ferrari was unstoppable. Michael Schumacher had won his first five races of the season, and the Ferrari-Schumacher dream team was expected to do the same at the Austrian Gran Prix. Ferrari's main competition came from BMW Williams, so it came as a surprise when his teammate, Rubens Barrichello, took pole position and lead for the entire race. That was until the final corner when the team pressured him to let Schumacher take the lead (the team order was banned by FIA the following year). Begrudgingly, Barrichello handed Schumacher the win but by just 0.182 seconds. In an act of chivalry, Schumacher insisted Barrichello take the top step on the step and even gave him the trophy, though this certainly broke protocol.

This wasn't the first time Schumacher and Barrichello had such a close race, nor was it the first time Ferrari had instructed Barrichello to hold back. Amid the pouring rain in the 2000 Canadian Grand Prix, Barrichello was closing in on Schumacher but, sticking to orders, flew over the line 0.174 seconds behind Schumacher.

In the 1954 French Grand Prix, the excitement was all about the much-anticipated arrival of the Mercedes W196 with its sleek stream-lined body and straight-8 fuel-injection engine. It was a demanding race, and only six cars would make it to the finish; both of those cars were Mercedes, with teammate Karl Kling giving Juan Manual Fangio in the W196 a 0.1-second lead to win. Sadly, this was another case of teams pressuring one driver to allow the other to maintain the lead.

The 0.1-second difference was again matched in the French Grand Prix seven years later. Phil Hill was in the lead until his Ferrari spun out of control. This allowed teammate Giancarlo Baghetti to beat Dan Gurney in his Porche by one-tenth of a second. On the other end of the scale, Jim Clark and his Lotus arrived an entire minute later.

A formation finish is when various cars from one team cross the line in formation, using extremely close to each other, such as the Ferrari 1-2-3 formation in 1965. What is commonly known as the 1-2-3-4 finish came at the 1969 Italian Grand Prix. The last lap of the race saw four drivers racing toward the finish line: Jackie Stewart, Jochen Rindt, Jean-Piere Beltoise, and Bruce McLaren. Stewart and Beltoise were on the same team in Matra. Rindt was driving a Lotus, and needless to say, McLaren was faithful to his car. All cars were constructed by Ford. Stewart crossed the line first, with Rindt just 0.8 seconds behind his tail. Beltoise and McLaren came in at 0.17 seconds and 0.19 seconds, respectively!

In 1982, Nelson Piquet and Riccardo Patrese both had to retire from the Austrian Grand Prix due to their Brabham BMW's mechanical issues. Alain Prost also had to retire with just 5 laps to go. This gave Elio de Angelis and Keke Rosberg a surprising opportunity to win their first Grand Prix. It was incredibly close, but de Angleis managed to cross the line 0.05 seconds ahead of Rosberg.

In 1986, the newly constructed Circuito de Jerez in Spain proved to be a spectacular race to see. Ayrton Senna and Nigel Mansell had managed to leave drivers like Nelson Piquet and Alain Prost behind. On the final corner, Mansell was able to pull out alongside Senna, but Senna kept his lead, winning by 0.14 seconds.

The penultimate of closest finishes takes us back to Schumacher and Barrichello in the 2002 US Grand Prix. Because Schumacher had secured his fifth world championship, Barrichello was not pressured to let his teammate win. In a Ferrari-style show of dominance, it is supposedly said that the two would cross the finish line together, but after pulling out of the last corner side-by-side, Schumacher slowed down a fraction. This was just enough for Barrichello to take the lead by 0.011 seconds. Another act of chivalry?

Only one other race comes close to what was potentially a farcical 0.011 seconds between Schumacher and Barrichello, but we will never know whether it can be classed as the closest race ever. That's because, in the 1971 Italian Grand Prix, only two decimal places were used in timing. Because the championship had already been decided, this was the perfect race to give some new drivers a chance to demonstrate their skills. By lap 16, both Ferraris had retired, and the race began to break into packs. The leading pack contained Mike Hailwood, making his debut along with François Cevert, Ronnie Peterson, Jo Siffert, Howden Ganley, Chris Amon, Peter Gethin, and Jackie Oliver. It's worth noting that Jackie Oliver and Mike Hailwood had pole positions 13 and 18, respectively. After lap 45, Amon was out, and between the remaining drivers, any one of them could see the checkered flag and seal their first Grand Prix win. As it happened, the infamous Parabolica corner was enough to give Gethin enough of a lead to win by 0.01 seconds.

While on the subject of close finishes, it's only fair that the qualifying race for the last European Grand Prix in 1997 is mentioned. Just 14 minutes into the qualifying race,

Jacques Villeneuve set a lap time of 1:21.072, and fourteen minutes later, Michael Schumacher hit exactly the same lap time. As if that wasn't enough, there were 9 minutes to go before the end of the session when Heinz-Harald Frentzen crossed the finish line with a time of 1:21.072. This was the first time in Formula 1 history that the same lap time had been set not just twice but three times.

7

A SERIES OF UNFORTUNATE
EVENTS THAT COST A TITLE

"No driver fought harder to get into Formula One racing and few fought harder when they got there. Hugely determined, immensely aggressive, and spectacularly darling, he was one of the most exciting drivers ever to race."

— FORMULA ONE HALL OF FAME

Formula 1's Hall of Fame is referring to Nigel Mansell.[1] When you consider the great Formula 1 drivers, especially those from Britain, the mind will probably jump to Lewis Hamilton. He is, after all, not only one of the greatest Formula 1 drivers in history, but on paper, he is also the greatest British driver. Before looking at Mansell as one of motor sporting legends, let's consider some of the differences that make these two drivers incomparable.

Due to the intensity of racing, drivers like Hamilton have an extensive team behind them beyond mechanics. It's not uncommon for drivers to have a physiotherapist, fitness trainer, and even a nutritionist. The emphasis on physical health that today's drivers have seen is largely due to the struggles previous drivers endured. Mansell didn't have the same support or technology for that matter!

The likes of Nigel Mansell should be celebrated for his use of both head and heart and his dedication to a sport that many today wouldn't consider participating in. His perseverance will always be remembered.

Mansell was born in August 1953 near Birmingham. He was driving before the age of eight and found inspiration in Jim Clark, especially the 1962 British Grand Prix. His first racing experience was in kart racing, which led to a move to Formula Ford. Even though he was successful, his father disapproved. By 1977, Mansell was the British Formula Ford champion. That same year, Mansell broke his neck in a testing accident, and doctors told him he wouldn't drive again. Rather than listening to his doctor's recommendations, he told nurses he was going to the toilet and then slipped out of the hospital.

To finance his move to Formula Ford, Mansell had already sold most of his belongings. After this incident, he and his wife had to sell their house and use the money to enter Formula 3 racing. It was a big risk; in 1979 he crashed again, badly enough to break his vertebrae. The painkillers helped hide the true extent of his injuries, which was enough to get him onto the Formula 1 team test driving for Lotus.

Over the next few years, Mansell grew very close to Colin Chapman, the head of Lotus. Chapman's sudden death in 1982 was too much for Mansell, and two years later, he moved to William-Honda. He had a slow start with the team. Of the 71 Grand Prix starts, he didn't win a single one. That changed in the 1985 European Grand Prix, sealing his first win and then going on to win 11 races in 18 months. The Australian Grand Prix was looking to be the race that would finally win him the world championship.

Teams and drivers were tired. The schedule over the previous months had been hectic, and even Mansell admitted that he would be glad when the weekend was over. Adelaide was the first time a Brit had made it into the championship equation. Alain Prost and Nelson Piquet were also in the running. Mansell was on 70 points, Prost 64, and teammate Piquet was just one point behind Prost. For Mansell to take home the championship, he only needed to come in third! Piquet and Prost both needed a win.

This wasn't any reassurance for Mansell. Piquet had successfully won two World Championships at the last race of the season. Also racing were the likes of Ayrton Senna, René Arnoux, and Keke Rosberg. Nothing was in the bag, and Mansell's attitude was that settling with third place wasn't enough. He was out to win! His determination led him to the pole position after completing three consecutive and impressive laps at 1:19.7, 1:19.1, and 1.19.4. Piquet took second place just 0.311 seconds behind him in the sessions. In third place on the grid, Senna sat in his Lotus, and behind him, Prost in his McLaren.

The track was a cause for concern. Heavy rain days before meant the track was particularly oily and had no grip. Conditions changed frequently, but most drivers opted for soft tires. During the sessions, there were several bumps and scrapes, but morning and afternoon laps could go differently. None of this was going to phase Mansell or shift his winning mentality.

Mansell got off to an excellent start, but the first lap saw things rapidly change for the Brit. Senna, who thrived on wet tracks, took the lead on the first corner; next came Piquet and then Rosberg! Piquet took the lead, giving the crowd three different leaders in a matter of miles. Relief for Mansell came on lap 23 when Piquet spun off. Then, it seemed like Prost's race was ruined when his front tire got a puncture. However, the Goodyear technicians found the tire to be in good condition and informed the other teams that the drivers wouldn't need to stop for new tires. This would prove to be fatal for Mansell's chances of winning!

On lap 63, Rosberg heard a loud noise from the back of the car and assumed the engine had failed. After pulling over to the side of the track, he saw that the right rear tire had suffered delamination (when the tread separates from the casing). Contrary to what Goodyear's technicians had thought, the tires weren't lasting the race.

Mansell was already heading for Dequetteville Terrace when his left rear tire disintegrated into thin air! The entire left rear corner of the car broke up, and Mansell was thrown into never-ending swerves and twitches. In what can only be called pure skill, Mansell managed to keep the car under control, considering what could have happened. Few drivers can come through a 200-mile-per-hour blowout unhurt. Mansell was known for his hot temper, but rather than jumping out of his car in a fit of rage, he sat there for a few minutes, probably taking in the fact that his chance of championship had disappeared as quickly as his tire.

Mansell was lucky to be alive, and Goodyear pulled the other drivers straight in for a tire change. The end result was Prost having no competition and breezing over the finish line to gain the 9 points he needed for the championship. At the end of the season, Alain finished with 72 points and Mansell with 70.

The irony continues! Mansell's skillful handling of the car led to no crash. If there had been one, it would have been likely that the red flag would have been raised and the race called to a stop. Had that happened, Mansell would have had the points to celebrate the championship.

Mansell's career was epic. Of his 192 races (187 starts), he won 31 races—a British record only beaten by Hamilton. His daring driving style saw 32 accidents, 30 fastest laps, and 59 podium appearances. His personality didn't always win him friends in the racing world, but his talent was well respected. After his win in Adelaide, Prost made a point of recognizing how Mansell deserved the 1986 title and just how much class he had in and out of the car.

8

FORMULA 1'S GREAT COMEBACK

"Giving up is something a Luda doesn't do. I always go extreme ways"[1]

— NIKI LAUDA

Rocket speeds, hot car parts, and explosive fuel are the perfect recipe for fires, and the risk is only increased if there is an impact. Some don't make it out alive, others go on to inspire.

In 1967, Lorenzo Bandini clipped a chicane, his car flipped, caught on fire, and then set fire to the nearby straw bales lining the track. It's impossible to imagine the conscious driver's pain as people attempted to pull him out of the car. He died three days later.

Footage from 1971 shows smoke billowing from the flame-engulfed car of Jo Siffert[2]. The crash not only caused a fire but also left the Swiss driver trapped in the cockpit. Although it was a non-championship race, it still highlights the risk the sport carries.

Other accidents have left drivers with horrific injuries but spared them their lives. With regards to burns, it was Nigel Mansell's debut Formula 1 appearance that left him with first and second-degree burns. Fuel had spilled into the cockpit, but in his own words, he "had reached the point, the very minute I had worked toward all my life- and there I was getting my arse burned!"[3] When offered the chance not to start, Mansell refused, and after mechanics splashed him with water, he left the grid. Mansell made it around 40 laps before engine issues caused him to retire, but the pain he must have endured must have been unbearable.

Considering the accident-prone career of Mansell, he did have some amazing comebacks, but there is a hero who inspired some of today's Formula 1 top names. To become the best of the best in a sport riddled with danger, you need to have more than skill. If it hadn't been for Niki Lauda's raw determination, he may never have been able to become a three-time World Champion.

Niki Lauda was born in Vienna, Austria in 1949. His family ran a paper manufacturing company and were considerably well off; however, they didn't support Lauda's interest in racing as they had hoped he would follow his father into the family business. His only interest in the business was driving the delivery trucks and the forklifts around the factories. His racing debut hit the papers in 1968, and in 1968, he began racing for Formula Vee. By that point, his relationship with his parents had become tenser than ever.

In order to enter Formula 1 and race for Max Mosley and the March team, Lauda had to secure a $158,700 loan. Unfortunately, even though the bank had agreed to the loan, his grandfather was on the board of the Austrian bank, and he vetoed it, saying that no member of the Lauda family would ever own a racing car.

Some would have taken this as a sign, but not Lauda. Instead, he managed to secure a loan against his own life insurance. It was a gamble that paid off. His first Grand Prix was in Austria in 1971; his first Grand Prix points came two years later in Belgium. In later years, Lauda said that his fight with his grandfather not only gave him the freedom to do what he wanted to do but also gave him the kick to succeed.[4]

It was in 1974 that Lauda's Formula 1 career grew further when he joined Ferrari. That year, he won his first Grand Prix in Spain and ended the season in fourth place, a spectacular setup for the season ahead. The 1975 season saw Lauda win in Monaco, Belgium, Sweden, France, and the U.S. As Lauda's success grew, his parents came around to his racing career. His grandfather didn't live long enough to see it.

Of all the racing seasons, 1976 could be one of the most talked about. Out of the first nine races, Lauda won five and already had more than double the points of his closest competitors. He was 31 points ahead and ready to defend his title. The 10th race was scheduled for the notoriously dangerous Nürburgring track in Germany.

The track in a small town called Nürburg is located in the Eifel Mountain area, which explains the 1000-foot (300-meter) elevation. The course has numerous twists and turns that appear out of nowhere. Of the 170 tight corners around the track, around 90% are blind! The Flugplatz, Brunnchen, and Pflanzgarten sections of the track are known areas for cars to visibly leave the ground. G-Forces are exceptionally strong at the Fox Hole section after five extensive corners, with the last ending in a steep downhill and immediate uphill drive. The track, nicknamed "The Green Hell" by Jackie Stewart, has claimed the lives of 70 amateur and professional motorsport drivers since its construction in 1927.

Prior to the race, Lauda encouraged other drivers to boycott the German Grand Prix because of safety concerns. Regrettably, he was outvoted, and the race went ahead. Lauda made it to the second lap when he lost control of his Ferrari and crashed into a wall. The car caught on fire as it bounced back across the track. Lauda was stuck in around 800-degree heat for approximately 50 seconds. Two cars hit the burning Ferrari, and one just skimmed past; all drivers attempted to save him but couldn't.

It was the actions of Arturo Merzario that saved Lauda's life. Merzario stopped his Wolff and single-handedly managed to pull Lauda from the flames. Lauda suffered from first, second, and third-degree burns over his entire body, with his wrist and head with the worst burns. He had several broken bones, and his lungs were damaged from the toxic fumes. Merzario told reporters, "Niki was lucky because the pain of the planes and the gas fumes made him pass out."[5] Lauda fell into a coma, and at one point, a priest was called to administer his last rites. But his survival was only half the miracle!

It took Lauda just 6 weeks to recover enough to race again. In that time, he had only missed two races. This phenomenal comeback in the Italian Gran Prix gave a bloody and bandaged Lauda a fourth-place finish. His rival and winner of the German Grand Prix, James Hunt, went on to win the championship, with Lauda finishing the season one point behind him.

Lauda's accident proved that the track was too dangerous, and Formula 1 has never raced there since. One new rule implemented some years later was a helicopter within 1 minute of any on-track accident, unlike the 5 to 6 minutes it took the helicopter to reach Lauda.

Lauda retired in 1979 but was tempted back in by McLaren in 1982. His second retirement from racing was in 1985. Missing half an ear and scars across his face, it was his trademark red cap that people would notice as he still hung around the tracks. He became a Non-Executive Chairman on the Mercedes board and played a significant role in convincing Lewis Hamilton to join the team, and the two remained close until his death in 2019. Sadly, his health was still suffering from the severe injuries he sustained in the fire.

He was the heart and hero of Formula 1. He was a resolute fighter and inspired not only racing drivers but anyone who heard his story. While drivers could learn from his wealth of experience, everybody can learn from his words of wisdom!

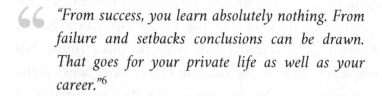

"From success, you learn absolutely nothing. From failure and setbacks conclusions can be drawn. That goes for your private life as well as your career."[6]

— NIKI LAUDA

9

TRAGEDY ON THE TRACK

> *"If a person has no dreams, they no longer have any reason to live."*[1]
>
> — AYRTON SENNA

In terms of Formula 1 history, there is one Grand Prix that should never be forgotten as fans watched one of its heroes die in front of them. Before unveiling the events that led up to this tragedy, respect should be paid to the dozens of lives lost in one race that perhaps only our grandparents might remember today. Whether a single death in a race or dozens, each tragedy on the track highlights certain safety failures throughout the history or Formula 1.

The 24 Hours of Le Mans is an endurance race first held in 1923. The winner is the driver who covers the most distance in 24 hours. Just because the race is one of distance, it doesn't mean speeds are slower, with average speeds well over 200 miles per hour.

On June 11th, 1955, 60 cars lined up for the start of the race. Formula 1 names at the start of the race included Juan Manuel Fangio, Stirling Moss, Mike Hawthorn, and Luigi Musso. Fangio and Moss were racing for Mercedes, as was Pierre Levegh, an elder statesman of French motor racing. At the end of the 35th lap, Lance Macklin braked a little too hard in his Austin-Healey, causing the car to veer into the path of Levegh. Levegh had time to raise a hand to warn Fangio of the danger, who was just behind him. This was enough to save Fangio, but it was too late for Levegh. At 150 miles per hour, the right front wheel of his Mercedes rode onto the rear wheel of Austin-Healey.

The car flew into the air, crashing into the embankment and disintegrating. Debris from the car, including the engine, radiator, and front suspension, was scattered into the crowd as the car, made of magnesium alloy, exploded into flames. High-speed projectiles wiped out those standing on ladders to get a better view. Carnage and chaos descended as the race continued.

Levegh died on impact. Hawthorn pulled into the pits in tears at the tragedy that had been unveiled. Though reports vary, the number of spectators who lost their lives was between 80 and 84 with another 120 to 170 people injured[2]. Questions were raised as to why Mercedes didn't pull their remaining drivers out as a sign of respect, but it wasn't that simple. To retire the team, all of the highest directors had to be contacted and agree.

More questions were raised as to why the entire race wasn't called, but Le Mans organizers justified their actions. The crowd was anywhere from 250,000 to 300,000 people, many of whom were unaware of what had happened. If the race had been canceled, panic and mass exit may have occurred, hindering the ability of emergency services to do their jobs. In hindsight, had this happened, the death toll and injuries could have been higher.

To date, this is motor racing's most tragic day, and lessons were learned. But this didn't stop more tragedies on the Formula 1 tracks.

Disaster struck the 1994 San Marino Grand Prix even before the race. During the qualifying session on Friday, Rubens Barrichello clipped a curb at 140 miles per hour, throwing the car into the air and then rolling several times before coming to a standstill upside down. Barrichello's tongue blocked his airway, but Sid Watkins, the FIA doctor, saved his life before being airlifted to hospital. Senna was at his bedside when he regained consciousness.

The next day, Austrian driver, Roland Ratzenberger went over a curb in his Simtek-Ford, but he continued instead of heading to the pits. On the next lap, the car's front wing snapped off, and he was left unable to steer or brake. There were no tire barriers at this curve, so the Austrian racer, in his first Formula 1, slammed straight into a concrete wall. Senna jumped straight into a course car and headed for the scene of the crash.

Doctors attempted to treat him before he was taken to the same hospital as Barrichello the day before. Doctors discovered he had received three fatal injuries and had died on impact. Once again, Senna was there at the hospital. This was the first Formula 1 death since Riccardo Paletti at the 1982 Canadian Grand Prix. Despite this, the race went following day's race went ahead, and Ratzenberger's grid spot was left empty as a sign of respect.

Prior to the actual Formula 1 race, Senna raised safety concerns, feeling that the pace car of the formation lap was only a publicity stunt for Porsche. Senna decided to meet with other drivers in the hope of reestablishing the Grand Prix Driver's Association, even offering to lead the association in the hope of improving Formula 1 safety. What happened in the race that followed only highlighted the need for this.

On the very first lap, Pedro Lamy, driving for Lotus, crashed into the back of JJ Lehto's Benetton. The colliding cars caused debris to fly into the crowd, injuring nine people. For 5 laps, drivers followed the safety car until the race resumed. It only took one more lap for Senna to enter a corner at 192 miles per hour. He braked hard and hit a concrete wall unprotected by tires at 131 miles per hour. With the front right wheel and nose cone torn off, Senna sat there motionless. The only sign of hope was a slight lift of his head before it dropped back down again.

Sid Watkins, who had suggested that Senna not race, was there to secure his airway and do everything he could to save Senna's life. All of this was broadcast live around the world. Senna was pronounced dead later that afternoon. He suffered from three fatal injuries, any one of which could have caused his death. During the examination of Senna's car, an Austrian flag was found inside, a planned tribute to Ratzenberger.

It would have been horrendous for fans, friends, and family members to have witnessed these accidents, but there were still drivers in the race, even teammates. Incredibly, the race was not called off. Technically, neither driver died on the track, even though Senna's autopsy put his time of death at shortly after the crash. Under Italian law, the race was to continue. Senna's teammate, Damon Hill, managed to come in 6th, but Ratzenberger's teammate, David Brabham, spun off on the 27th lap. Either way, it's hard to imagine their fallen teammates would have been anything but proud of their emotional endurance.

Changes were made. Niki Lauda took on Senna's mission and reformed the Grand Prix Drivers' Association along with Michael Schumacher. Massive safety changes followed with improved crash barriers, tracks being redesigned, and higher safety standards.

Senna was a Brazilian (and worldwide) hero. Even Tina Turner had dedicated her song "Simply the Best" to him the previous year.[3] The Brazilian government declared 3 days of mourning after his death. Three million people lined the streets of Sao Paulo, with Alain Prost, Jackie Stewart, Damon Hill, and Rubens Barrichello all attending the funeral as pallbearers.

Schumacher went on to win the race and that year's championship, but the season will always be remembered as the saddest of Formula 1. At the next Formula 1 race, two grid spots were left empty; the only thing replacing the cars was a Brazilian and Austrian flag.

10

FATHER AND SON RACING

> "I am a firm believer that genetics are quite a big part of this...I would probably say 66 percent genetic, 33 percent nurtured."[1]
>
> — NICO ROSBERG

Can motor racing skills be passed down from one generation to the next? That answer depends on who you ask. If it's the likes of Niki Lauda, he would most certainly say that racing success has nothing to do with the genes, considering the absolute lack of support he received. Lewis Hamilton would agree. Hamilton's parents were fully supportive, but in terms of inherited skills, nobody else in the Hamilton family raced cars. On the contrary, a few examples of father and son duos have demonstrated something to be said for having both support and a leading role model.

Nico Rosberg had a stellar example of a role model in the world of Formula 1. His father, Keke Rosberg, raced from 1978 to 1986. Of his 130 races and 114 starts, he won 5 races and made it to the podium 17 times. It took Keke Rosberg 4 years to experience his first Grand Prix win. In 1982, he won the Swiss Grand Prix, the Monaco Grand Prix the following year, and 1984 the Dallas Grand Prix. In 1985, he won both the Detroit and Australian Grand Prix. It was in 1982 that Keke Rosberg managed to take home the season championship even though he had only won one race. The year prior to his retirement, Nico was born.

At the age of 6, Nico was behind the wheel of a kart. Both parents encouraged his enthusiasm on the condition that his schoolwork didn't suffer. Nico was quick to learn both behind his desk and the wheel. His linguistic skills are impressive; he speaks English, German, French, Italian, and Spanish. Keke Rosberg became his son's manager, and he quickly moved up the ranks in kart racing. Nico's rivalry with Lewis Hamilton actually began when the teens were in Formula A karting. Nico joined the Williams Formula 1 team in 2006.

During his career, Nico Rosberg spent his first 4 seasons with Williams before moving to Mercedes in time to experience their V6 turbo-hybrid dominance. Younger Rosberg won 23 Grand Prix and appeared on the podium 57 times. In 2016, younger Rosberg and Hamilton had been battling for the championship, and the penultimate race put Roseberg 5 points ahead. Lewis Hamilton won the Abu Dhabi Grand Prix, but Rosberg came in second, securing the World Championship. After achieving his dream, Rosberg shocked fans and retired.

Keko and Nico Rosberg were the second father and son duo to both win a World Championship. The first to do so were the Hills, but not without a tragedy that will unfold soon.

Giles Villeneuve made his Formula 1 debut in 1977 after a career in racing snowmobiles. He joined McLaren for the British Grand Prix, and then he went to drive for Ferrari for the rest of the season, where he stayed until 1982. He won 6 Grand Prix and was so close to the championship title in 1979, missing out by 5 points. Statistics weren't in Villeneuve's favor, but fellow drivers admired his "god-given" talent. Sadly, Villeneuve died in a high-speed collision in the 1982 Belgian Grand Prix qualifiers; his son Jacques was just 11 years old at the time.

In Jacques Villeneuve's younger years, he and his family had traveled to different races to watch his father. Troubles in the marriage led his father to stay away from the family home. At the time of his death, his son hadn't seen him in 2 years. Jacques felt that, sadly, it was a good thing that he passed away because he became the man of the family, which gave him the strength to become the racer he did.

Jacques began racing at the age of 15 under the guidance of his uncle with the same name. He won 11 Grand Prix races and has had many successes in others, making him a racing hero for Canada. He is one of five drivers to win both the Formula One Crown and the Indy 500 and one of four drivers to win the Formula 1 World Championship and the Indy World Championship. He won the championship in 1997. It was only his second season.

When it comes to the Schumachers, there isn't just one father and son pair but two, making for competitive talk around the table at all family occasions. Brothers Michael and Ralf both had sons who made their own names on the track. Michael Schumacher won the 91 Grand Prix and 7 World Championships in his 20-year career, but in 2013, he suffered a skiing accident. Two years later, his son Mick began a career in Formula 4. In 2021, he made his Formula 1 debut with Ferrari. Though he hasn't won any races, it's still early days.

Mick's cousin David Schumacher is the son of Michael's younger brother. David raced in 2020 in Formula 3, but in 2022, he had an accident that fractured a lumbar vertebra. Again, being younger than his cousin, there is still the possibility of a fruitful career ahead.

The Piquets also have more than one generational connection. Nelson Piquet has 7 children. Geraldo, Pedro

Estácio, Marco, and Laszlo are active in racing. His daughter Julia was a kart racer, and his younger daughter Kelly was involved in Formula 3. Nelson Angelo Tamsma Piquet Souto Maior (better known as Nelson Piquet Jr.) has reached the greatest fame of all the children.

Nelson Piquet began his Formula 1 career in 1978, and between then and his retirement in 1991, he entered 207 races with 204 starts and won 23 races with 60 podium performances. He also won the championships in 1981, 1983, and 1987. Aside from his racing achievements, he was also known for his rather loose tongue. In just one magazine appearance, he named Nigel Mansell an "uneducated blockhead" whose wife was "ugly." He labeled Senna "gay," and Enzo Ferrari was apparently "senile."[2]

His son, Nelson Piquet Jr., could have had more success. Piquet Jr. won 2 races in Formula E, made 5 podium appearances, and became the first Formula E champion. His Formula 1 career had ended rather abruptly after the 2008 Singapore debacle. Interestingly enough, his father's inability to control his mouth may have been what helped that controversial race to come to light!

With the exception of the Schumachers and Nelson Piquet Jr., it's clear how motor racing advancements have led to younger generations achieving more than their fathers. Nothing could be truer in the case of the Verstappen family. Jos Verstappen raced for 8 Formula 1 seasons, retiring in 2003. From his 106 starts, he scored only seven times. Perhaps this is a case of "those who can't do, teach."

Jos Verstappen's son Max was born in 1997. Max's mother was a successful kart driver. Max Verstappen won his 6th Formula 3 race and the next 6 races at the age of 16. That same year, he joined the Red Bull Junior Team, ready to join Formula 1 in 2015. That season, Max became the youngest driver to compete in a Grand Prix, and the year after, he became the youngest driver to win a Gran Prix. By 2022, this young driver had won his second World Championship and entered the Formula 1 drivers top 10.

The Verstappens are certainly hitting the news right now, but prior to this, there was another record-breaking father-and-son motor racing relationship that was perhaps the most famous father-and-son duo in Formula 1 history that ended in a tragedy of a different kind.

Graham Hill didn't pass his driving test until he was 24 years old. He certainly entered motor racing later than most. Not only that, but Hill was also taking the UK unemployment benefits when he managed to get a job as a mechanic at a racing school. Colin Chapman spotted Hill's talent, and in 1958, he became a Formula 1 driver. By 1975, Graham Hill had won 14 Grand Prix with 36 podium appearances. He won the World Championship in 1962 and 1968. Hill earned the nickname "Mr. Monaco" after winning the Monaco Grand Prix five times and reached legendary status after winning the triple crown (the Monaco Grand Prix, the Indy 500, and the 24 Hours Le Mans) in 1972.

Graham's son, Damon, was just 2 years old when his father won his first championship. Growing up, Damon must have known the danger his father faced every time he raced. Unlike many other young Formula 1 prodigies, Damon didn't lose his father on the track. Instead, Graham Hill died in a plane accident in 1975.

Williams took Damon on as a test driver but not because of his raw talent. He had not had much success in Formula 3000 or Formula 3, but he showed fierce determination and worked hard, much like his father. It wasn't until 1992 that Damon made his Formula 1 debut. The following years saw Nigel Mansell retire, Alain Prost retire, and then the sad passing of Ayrton Senna, leaving Damon to lead the team.

Despite his slow start, Damon went on to win 22 Grand Prix and the World Champion title in 1996. This made the Hills the first father and son duo to both have the title. Damon Hill was knighted in 1997. On what would have been Graham Hill's 94th birthday, his son revealed that his father was due to receive an OBE (Officer of the Most Excellent Order of the British Empire awarded for outstanding contributions), which would have given the pair another momentous achievement in common.

As the next generation of drivers takes to the tracks, those fortunate enough to be around can take pride in the fresh talent. The only thing now is to watch and see if a third generation catches the racing bug and the grandchildren carry on the legacies.

11

POLE POSITION MIGHT NOT BE EVERYTHING

> *"Teo liked to drive with a lot of precision, which pays off in the quick corners...But he needed unbroken concentration to do it. That was his downfall."*[1]
>
> — PAT SYMONDS

The origins of the term pole position didn't begin with motor racing. In horse racing, the horse that was fastest in the qualifier race got to start the race on the inner part of the course, next to the pole. In both sports, pole position is the most sought-after place to be at the beginning of a race.

The statistics help to see why drivers have their hearts set on this prime spot. Forty percent of Formula 1 drivers who start in the pole position go on to win the race.[2] Pole position gives a driver both a strategic and psychological advantage.

Drivers have practice sessions on a Friday. Free Practice 1 (FP1) and Free Practice 2 (FP2) last an hour each, and FP3 is saved for Saturday morning. On Saturday afternoon, the stakes are raised in three qualifying sessions: Q1 lasts 18 minutes, Q2 for 15 minutes, and Q3 is just 12 minutes. The driver who scores the fastest lap in Q3 takes the pole position, and the rest of the drivers form in respective of their lap time.

Pole position will also be on the ideal line to the first corner, which can be to the left or the right, depending on the direction of that first corner. The starting grid leads to a bottleneck of 20 powerful cars and their skilled drivers screeching off their grid position into practically a single file. The driver in pole position is first out of the bottleneck, leaving his competitors fighting for the next best position. To start a race like this means the driver doesn't have to concentrate on the tactics of passing other drivers. All they have to think about is the road ahead. A lead in the beginning is much easier to keep, at least in the first few laps, giving the driver a much-needed boost of confidence that can help with the rest of the race.

Pole position can be even more critical on certain tracks. Monaco is renowned for its difficulty. Out of the entire track, there is really only one chicane where overtaking is possible. The winner of the Monaco Grand Prix is almost exclusively the driver who starts in pole position. Ayrton Senna is a prime example, holding the record for most wins at Monaco with six. Senna had five pole positions at this track, another record.

That's not to say anything less than pole position means no chance of winning. Many drivers have been in last position and ended up winning a race. Tracks have become a more even playing field over the decades, but psychologically, an empty track ahead will still feel great. Despite what the statistics say, pole position hasn't always done one driver any favors.

Teo Fabi was born in Milan in 1955. While studying mechanical engineering, he raced motorbikes. In 1976, he made the switch to cars and quickly made his way through Formula Ford 1600, European Formula 3, and Formula 2. By 1982, he was driving in Formula 1 with Toleman. He scored no points in his first season, so he briefly went into CART (Championship Auto Racing Teams) and just missed out on the title. In 1984, he returned to Formula 1 and continued his CART career.

Fabi secured his first pole position in the 1985 German Grand Prix and the only pole position for the Toleman team. This was impressive for two reasons. Toleman hadn't started in the front four rows all season, and the team had missed the first three races. Also, during the qualifying session, Fabi crashed on the wet track and had a decent smack to his head, enough to not even remember where he had qualified. Fabi lost the lead on the 1st lap and, by lap 29, retired due to clutch issues.

The following year, Fabi would again reach pole position in the Austrian Grand Prix, now racing with Benetton. In second position was Gerhard Berger racing on home ground. Five of the six grid positions behind them were filled with what could only be described as the Formula 1 "walk of fame" of the 80s, with Keke Rosberg, Alain Prost, Nigel Mansell, Nelson Piquet, and Ayrton Senna.

As soon as the race began, Berger took the lead over Fabi and Prost, Mansell, and Piquet passed Rosberg and Ricardo Patrese. On lap 17, Fabi regained the lead, only for his engine to fail seconds later, and he was forced to retire. The 1985 retirement was due to a mechanical fault and perhaps a rather inexperienced team, but the Benetton engine's mechanical errors were certainly unfortunate.

In the same year at the Italian Grand Prix, the grid looked similar, with the who's who of racing in the leading positions, but Fabi was in the pole position. Unfortunately, the formation lap led to a disaster, and after his engine stalled, he lost his pole position and went to the back of the grid. After setting his fastest lap, he retired because of a puncture.

Fabi was a sensible driver who was as cool as a cucumber at high speeds. What he lacked in height, he made up for with inner strength. He was quick and precise around corners and "deserved better," according to Pat Symonds, engineer for Toleman and later Benetton[3].

In his 5 seasons, Fabi participated in 71 Grand Prix with 64 starts. His bad luck with mechanics led to just two podium appearances and 23 career points. His racing career wasn't limited to Formula 1, and he wasn't afraid to enter different races, from the 24 Hours of Le Mans to the Indy 500. However, he may always remain most famous for his three pole positions that never led to a lead.

12

FROM THE CLOSEST FINISH TO THE GRAND PRIX THAT LEFT EVERYONE WAITING

"The man with natural ability uses finer limits than a man who has none. It is like a born artist being able to place paint on a canvas and make it a picture, whereas the majority of us would only make a mess. For I consider motor racing an art."[1]

— JIM CLARK

Two of the closest Formula 1 wins came down to 0.01 of a second, but what about the other extreme? Imagine watching a gripping Formula 1 race only to have enough time to boil the kettle and make your favorite hot drink between the first driver to cross the winning line and the second! This is the reason why many feel Jim Clark was the greatest Formula 1 driver of all time!

Jim Clark, born in 1936, was the youngest of five children. His family were farmers; considering his older siblings were all girls, he was expected to grow up and take over the farm. His family was less than pleased about his passion for racing. In 1958, Clark came second in the Brands Hatch GT race behind Colin Chapman, founder of Lotus. Chapman invited Clark to join the Formula Junior team, and he won his first race.

By the end of the 1960 season, he was promoted to Formula 1 with Lotus, but one weekend at the Spa-Francorchamps circuit almost led to him giving up racing altogether. In the Belgium Grand Prix, racer Chris Bristow had a fatal crash and got thrown from his car. Clark only just managed not to hit Bristow's body. If that wasn't enough, a friend and teammate, Alan Stacey, was hit in the face by a bird. He spun out of control, crashed, and died, all just a few laps after Bristow's accident. The following year pushed him over the edge that much further. Through no fault of Clark's, his Lotus and Wolfgang von Trips Ferrari collided, and von Trap did not make it out alive. The car hit the crowd, killing 14 spectators. It was Chapman who convinced Clarke to stay.

The 1962 season was when Clarke began to shine. Between his driving skills and the design talents of Chapman, nearly all of their losses could be attributed to a mechanical fault. That year, Clark missed out on the championship title because of an oil leak, and the next three seasons would seem like an ironic circle of events.

In 1963, he won his first championship; in 1964, he missed out on the championship because of another oil leak. In 1965, he won his second championship and the Indy 500. In his 6 years of Formula 1 career, he entered 73 races and started 72. He had 25 wins, 33 pole positions, and 32 podium appearances. He also holds the record for the highest percentage of laps in the lead position in one season and the highest possible championship points for seasons 1963 and 1965—all for Lotus. It's understandable how he still holds the biggest winning margin.[2]

Damon Hill was having a terrible 1995 season. Though he had started strong, William and Michael Schumacher rose from behind to steal any hope of the championship. The final race was in Australia, and to end the season on a high, Hill had gained pole position with teammate David Coulthard behind him. Before the race began, 4 cars had already pulled out, and things got more interesting at the first pit stop. Coulthard underestimated the wet pit lane and, in what would today be a TikTok sensation, understeered straight into the pit lane wall. Roberto Moreno not only did the same but also in the same place. Schumacher and Jean Alesi clipped each, taking them both out. Nine drivers had retired by lap 29. Two engine failures and a gearbox failure allowed Hill to leave all this behind, leading Olivier Panis by two laps, a total of 2:55.713 minutes difference.

Juan Manuel Fangio had already won his second World Championship by the 1954 Italian Grand Prix, but that wouldn't let the Argentinian take his foot off the gas. Fangio was in his beloved Mercedes W196 and was in pole position, but it was close. He had beaten Alberto Ascari with Ferrari by just 0.2 seconds. The entire race was between Karl Kling, Stirling Moss, Ascari, and Fangio, each being in the lead at some point. On the 68th lap, Fangio led the Mercedes to a beautiful lead with an entire lap's difference, a rare occurrence in those times. Fangio achieved a 3:01.2-minute lead on Hawthorn.

In the second race of the 1967 season, Denny Hulme was 4th on the grid in Monaco. Ahead of him were Jack Brabham, Lorenzo Bandini, and John Surtees. Bandini soared into the lead, but the race was soon stopped due to Brabham's engine failure. Hulme and Jackie Stewart passed Bandini, but Stewart's engine failed, and this left Bandini chasing Hulme. Sadly, Bandini hit a pole coming into a chicane, flipping his car into the straw bales and catching fire. At this point, the mood was low, but drivers weren't aware that Bandini had lost his life. Hulme crossed the line first, his first-ever Grand Prix win, and the crowd had to wait 3:12.6 minutes for Graham Hill to take second place.

Jackie Stewart had won the first race of the 1969 season but did poorly in the Spanish qualifiers, leaving him 4th on the grid. The first lap saw him fall another two places behind, where he sat until lap 7. In a race that felt like the Formula 1 version of the Hare and the Tortoise, Stewart took lap 7 to lap 56 to overtake one car after the other. He took the lead from Chris Amon and, even more impressively, lapped Bruce McLaren twice. His winning margin was 3:59.6!

For the 1962 French Grand Prix, it looked like the title would be between Bruce McLaren, Graham Hill, and not-related Phil Hill. Jim Clark was in pole position, and Dan Gurney, who hadn't scored a point in the season yet, had qualified a full 1.7 seconds behind Clark. Hill led for most of the first 41 laps, but car troubles gave Gurney the lead. Between one car issue and another, Durney and his outstandingly powerful Porsche had no real competition. This wasn't just Gurney's first win. He won by a staggering 4:31.1 minutes.

One of Clark's finest records was the 1963 Belgian Grand Prix. Clark started 8th on the grid. He had gearbox troubles during the race, enough for him to drive one-handed with the other hand on the gearstick. The fact that he managed to take his Lotus to the lead position was a testimony of his skill. But, to lap every driver except Bruce McLaren and finish ahead of McLaren by 4:54 minutes.[3]

Clark's life was cut short suddenly in a 1968 Formula 2 race at the age of just 32. He had completed 7 seasons and achieved so much success in that short time. With more time, he would surely have convinced more people that he was the greatest Formula 1 driver!

HOW MANY TIMES HAVE YOU BEEN SURPRISED BY THE EXTREMES OF FORMULA 1 SO FAR?

"A lot of people criticize Formula 1 as an unnecessary risk. But what would life be like if we only did what was necessary?"[1]

— NIKI LAUDA

Sports teach adults and children so much. Today's attitude is that it's the participation that counts, and this is certainly true, but we can take more from sports than participation. It's about commitment, resilience, and how goals take time and effort to reach.

Personally, one of the greatest lessons we can all learn is by participating in sports, we can learn to face our fears, and of all those fears, it's the fear of failure that can hold us back from some of the greatest experiences in our lives.

Niki Lauda may not have reached the same Formula 1 status as the likes of Michael Schumacher, Ayrton Senna, Sebastian Vettel, and Lewis Hamilton, but the advice and wisdom that he passed on to drivers and non-drivers are mind-blowing.

Knowing that you were so close to death yet to still go back to the thing that almost killed you is one of the greatest fear-facing moments I could imagine. What was necessary for Lauda was to survive. But look at how much he would have missed out on in his life had he not taken what was for him, a necessary risk.

How much more fulfilling would all of our lives be if we took a leaf out of Lauda's book? But if stories like Lauda's aren't shared, how can people find their inspiration?

By sharing your views on Amazon, so many other people will be able to discover their own drive and motivation in challenging times.

I promise it only takes a couple of minutes, and I will be forever grateful! Now, let's get back to the race of extremes!

Scan the QR code below for a quick review!

13

WHAT TO DO WHEN YOU DON'T QUALIFY?

> *"You must always strive to be your best, but never believe that you are."*[1]

— JUAN MANUEL FANGIO

P eak tension during any Formula 1 weekend will be during Sunday's race; however, the pressure begins during the qualifying sessions. The fastest lap can secure pole position, but any breach of the rules, technical or behavior, and the driver receives penalties and has to move back on the grid. Only when the penalties are handed out are the grid spots finalized. Severe breaches of the rules can mean a driver is disqualified.

Another rule that leads to disqualification is the 107% rule. This rule states that drivers must set a lap within

107% of the fastest lap time. For example, if the fastest lap was 1:30, you would multiply this by 1.07 to get 1:391, so drivers must complete a lap within this time. The rule was introduced in 1996 to keep slower cars off the track. In some cases, drivers are still allowed to race from the back of the grid. This was the case the last time the 107% was implemented. In 2021, Lance Stroll failed to meet the time in the qualifiers, but he was allowed start the race from the back of the grid due to the times in his free practices.

The most recent rule change that could result in disqualification is the ban on porpoising. Porpoising is when a car bounces, but the wheels stay on the ground. It can be caused by the suspension, aerodynamics, or a bumpy track. Gone are the days when cars could clear the ground! It's a problem for two reasons. First, it's not good for the car, and second, the driver's health could be impacted. Lewis Hamilton, for example, has struggled with back pain because of bouncing in his Mercedes. FIA also recognizes that porpoising can distract drivers, making it a safety issue.

As of now, cars are monitored by a system called Aerodynamic Oscillation Metric (AOM).[2] The accelerometers on F1 cars can measure vertical oscillations. Free practice 3 is used to calculate the number of vertical oscillations, and ride height adjustments may have to be made. Adjusting the ride height will give the wheels more vertical room to absorb road shocks. If the ride height isn't adjusted by at least 10mm, the car won't pass the technical inspection, which could lead to disqualification.

Regardless of which sports you love, there will always be a few who are determined to break the rules and see if they can get away with it. With such vigilance today, this is much harder, but in the 70s, one particular driver loved to push all the limits.

The name Hans Heyer may not ring a bell in the Formula 1 world, but in racing, he achieved plenty. Heyer began in kart racing and made the switch to cars in 1970. During the 70s and 80s, he won the European Touring Car Championship, the Deutsche Rennsport Meisterschaft (DRM or German Racing Championship) three times, and had three consecutive wins in the Spa 24 hours. He also raced in the 24 Hours of Le Mans 12 times. In 1992, he even competed in the Nürburgring Truck Grand Prix. In German racing, he is a legend. In Formula 1, he is known for other reasons.

It was the 1977 German Grand Prix. There were 30 entries, including a newly formed ATS team. Despite his lack of experience driving single-seaters, Heyer was entered to drive for them. It was no surprise that he didn't make the qualifiers, but it must have been frustrating to find out that racing for his home country wouldn't be possible because of a few tenths of a second. Instead of getting angry, Heyer got cheeky!

There was a bit of mayhem at the grid because of a problem with the start lights. This allowed one of the German marshals, a friend of Heyer's, to sneak him onto the grid. The race finally got off to a start, as did Heyer. He made it around the first lap unnoticed. In fact, he made it around 9 laps before anyone discovered the extra car on the track, and only then because his gearbox failed. His retirement meant he didn't finish the race, and his antics caused him to be disqualified.

This makes Hans Heyer the only Formula 1 driver to achieve DNQ (did not qualify), DNF (did not finish), and DSQ (disqualified). He was banned from the next five Formula 1 races, which didn't seem to bother him too much as he wasn't planning to stay for another season.

Heyer isn't the only driver to have a rather amusing disqualification story. Al Pease was a British-Canadian driver who entered the Canadian Grand Prix in 1969. In what must have been a bit of a joke for spectators, Pease had an average speed of 43.1 miles per hour and was lapped 43 times by eventual winner Jack Brabham. This was a time when disqualification didn't even exist. Two years later, Pease qualified for the Canadian Grand Prix with a decent lap speed of 1:28.5, landing him position 17 on the grid. That would be the peak of his Grand Prix moment. He made it around 22 laps while those battling for the lead were on lap 46. After much protest, the black flag was raised, and Formula 1 had its first ever disqualification. The reason- driving too slow!

Disqualifications are not uncommon today, but the reasons seem a little bland, like breaking a weight limit or fuel restriction limit. Thanks to Heyer and Pease, we can appreciate a little humor and the lighter side of Formula 1!

14

DETERMINATION AT ITS BEST

"You don't expect to be at the top of the mountain the day you start climbing it."[1]

— RON DENNIS

It goes without saying that pushing a car on a Formula 1 track is highly dangerous and prohibited. At the same time, having a stopped car on the track can be equally dangerous. According to the International Sporting Code, a driver must move a car as soon as possible, and if they can't do it themselves, the marshals must assist. Whether the car can rejoin the race depends on one crucial factor. This can sometimes mean pushing a car back to the pits.

Aside from safety, there is another good reason why drivers are no longer tempted to push their cars. In 1961, the minimum car weight was 450 kilos, and by 2022, the minimum weight had increased to 798 kilos–still quite a difference, even for pushing![2]

The rules regarding pushing and disqualification weren't introduced until 1961, and just because all races were run under Formula 1 regulations in the 60s doesn't mean they all complied. Different tracks would allow you to get away with certain things that others wouldn't. This meant the 50s saw various attempts at pushing a car to the finish line, giving us two decades of extreme stories of drivers with willpower.

Stirling Moss was an exceptional driver, and being so close to a championship but never quite getting there must have been frustrating. The Brit turned that into grit as he pushed his car to the finish line not just once but twice! In the 1954 Italian Grand Prix, Juan Manuel Fangio had taken the checkered flag when Moss's car broke down near the finish line. The engine failure meant Moss had to push the car, albeit only for a few yards. The effort may not have been worth it, as Moss finished in 10th place. Moss was ahead by almost an entire lap at the Monaco Grand Prix the following year. On lap 80, his engine blew. He was 19 laps down, but pushing his car got him 9th place.

Jack Braham was another driver who pushed his car to the finish more than once. Braham was in 3rd place at the 1957 Monaco Grand Prix. The finish line was close, but unfortunately, the oil pump bracket of his Cooper fractured. Pushing his car allowed him to finish 6th, a whole 5 laps behind the winner, Juan Manuel Fangio. This might not sound like a big deal, but he managed this from the 15th place on the grid! What was more impressive was the 1959 US Grand Prix.

It was the season's penultimate race, and three of Formula 1's icons were in a close battle for the championship. Braham was in the lead with Moss 5.5 points behind him, and Tony Brooks was another 2.5 points behind Moss. Moss suffered a mechanical failure, and Brooks collided with Wolfgang von Trips; his race went downhill from there. His only real competition at this point was Bruce McLaren. On the final lap, the engine of Braham's Cooper just stopped. He pushed the car almost 400 yards to the finish line and then collapsed. At the end of the race, McLaren had won his first Grand Prix (the youngest winner at the time), and Braham secured himself as the world champion. Moss was one of the crowd that had surrounded Braham to congratulate him, and McLaren was forever grateful for Braham, saying he gifted him that race!

The year before had been a hard one for Formula 1, beginning with the French Grand Prix. Fangio had decided that this was his time to retire, and this race would be his last. Mike Hawthorn and his Ferrari teammate Luigi Musso had the best pole positions, but the qualifying sessions were overshadowed by Maurice

Trintignant, whose Cooper caught fire. Trintignant jumped out of his moving car and, although he suffered burns, could still race. The race itself is often remembered as the race where Musso flipped his Ferrari and sadly died later that day.

Peter Collins, Fangio, and Jean Behra were battling for second place, but Moss was able to slip past and seal 2nd place. When Behra retired, Wolfgang von Trips managed to take 3rd place. Had it not been for Collins running out of fuel, he would have made it into 4th place, but Fangio passed him. Collins pushed his Ferrari to the finish line. The fifth position was a great achievement, but what was more surprising was that he was still on the same lap as Hawthorn.

Fangio would remember Collins for a different reason. In 1956, Fangio and Collins were teammates in the Monza Grand Prix. In those days, drivers could still hand their car over to a teammate, and in an incredible act of sportsmanship, Collins handed his car over to Fangio. Fangio finished second in the race, and the teammates shared the points. When Collins gave his car to Fangio, he was effectively handing him the championship. Collins was only 24 at the time and assumed he would have more opportunities.

Despite many drivers pushing their cars in those days, not all finishes were counted. Behra finished his final 1957 French Grand Prix lap too slow because of a broken radiator, which was discounted. In the same 1959 race, when Braham pushed his way to the final, von Trips had a hole in his engine but took too long to push it to the finish line.

Bernard Collomb was the first to be disqualified for pushing his car in the 1961 German Grand Prix, but that's not to say others haven't been forgiven for pushing their cars. Thierry Bousten ran out of fuel in the 1985 San Marino Grand Prix. He was hoping to make it past the finish line but had to push the car for the last part and made it to 2nd place. Andrea de Cesaris was given a marshal's blessing to push his car to the line in the 1991 Mexico Grand Prix.

It may seem like an act of heroism and sheer determination to attempt to push a car to the finish line, but Nigel Mansell reminded drivers and teams why this is not a good idea and reinforced the already existing prohibition on pushing cars.

In 1984, the Grand Prix was held in Dallas. The weather was hotter than usual at a blazing 104°F. Many drivers had issues during the race because parts of the track were breaking up. Still, Mansell had earned his first-ever Grand Prix pole position and managed to keep the lead for the race's first half. During the race's second half, the conditions were getting to Mansell as he dropped into 5th place. Refusing to miss out on that potential championship point with 6th place, he began pushing his car after a minor hit with the wall led to gearbox damage. Between the heat and dehydration, Mansell collapsed next to his Lotus and had to be taken to a nearby medical center for treatment.

If a car engine stops, there can't be any assistance to restart the engine. In the case of Michael Schumacher in the 2003 European Grand Prix, a rear tire got stuck on gravel. Marshals were able to push the car, and as the engine hadn't stopped, Schumacher could join the race. In the case that an engine stops, the lap time doesn't count, despite the efforts to get the car back. With some luck, if marshals are pushing their car, the driver can push-start the car, which is accepted.

Of all the valiant attempts to push Formula 1 cars over the finish line, none will be remembered quite like Brabham. Not only did he mange to do this on more than one occasion but he also won races and earned the 1959 World Championship by doing so!

15

BUTTON'S ABILITY TO FACE THE MENTAL CHALLENGES OF FORMULA 1

> *"The fast, flowing parts, the high-speed corners, that's where a Formula One car is at its best-changes of direction, pulling high G-forces left and right."*[1]
>
> — JENSON BUTTON

The Canadian 2011 Grand Prix is remembered as Formula 1's longest race. For many drivers, it was a chaotic one, but for Jenson Button, he remembers it as his greatest race, not necessarily because he won but rather how he managed to win after so many setbacks!

Button was a hyperactive child who could only sit still when motor racing was on TV. His father supported his racing career, starting with kart racing. At 8 years old, he knew he wanted to be a Formula 1 driver. Just a few years later, Button won all 34 races in the British Cadet kart racing category. Ironically, Button failed his first road car driving test. The examiner was terrified by the speed at which Button passed through a narrow gap in traffic. That wouldn't stop him from going on to be the youngest winner of the European Formula Super A Championship at age 17!

The chance for Button to test Alain Prost's car was nothing short of a Christmas miracle. Frank Williams from Williams-BMW called Button when he was in a pub on Christmas Eve. Button's first season with Williams scored him another record, becoming the youngest driver to ever score points. But Button took the Formula 1 lifestyle a little too far. His Ferrari road car, 72-foot yacht, and a string of girlfriends didn't do his reputation much good. In 2003, Button had almost lost his career until BAR-Honda gave him the opportunity to revitalize his career, much to teammate Jacques Villeneuve's disgust. Villeneuve compared Button to a smiley boyband member. Nevertheless, Button recovered and got his first victory in the Hungarian Grand Prix in 2006.

Brawn GP was certainly not one of the well-known names in the Formula 1 circuit, which is why his 2009 season was a shocker! Brawn-Mercedes had a revamp and, along with Button, won the first six out of seven races. Button went on to win the championship, and Brawn picked up the Constructor's Championship. To everyone's surprise, Button decided to move to McLaren, becoming teammates with Lewis Hamilton.

Hamilton and Button had a friendly rivalry that would be tested in the 2011 Grand Prix in Montreal. Red Bull's Sebastian Vettel was in the pole position, followed by two Ferraris, another Red Bull, and then Hamilton. Button was starting in 7th position. The track was wet, but the worst was still to come, with heavy rain expected an hour into the race. Because of the standing water on the track, the race began behind the safety car for 5 laps!

Button had his first setback when Hamilton and Button touched cars; Hamilton hit the pit wall, trashing the right rear suspension and retiring. Button had a right rear puncture, leaving him in 14th place. After speeding behind the safety car, Button had to sit in the pits for his penalty, dropping him back to 15th. The drive penalty was a blessing in disguise for Button. His teammate's retirement had been playing on his mind, and hearing that Hamilton didn't blame him meant that Button could get his head back in the race. But this was to be short-lived.

The heavy rain caused a suspension of the race for over two hours. When the race finally restarted, Button had his second accident. He and Fernando Alonso attempted to take a corner in a chicane side-by-side, and their wheels touched. Button once again crawled back to the pit with another puncture and damage to the front wing. He was officially in last place.

At this point, many would have accepted that after two accidents, they were lucky to at least still be in the race—but not Button. Button had made 5 pit stops at this point, and the face of McLaren boss Ron Dennis said it all. He was stunned with one car out and the other last! Instead of defeat, Button decided that the only way was up!

What happened after lap 40 made this a race of extremes for Button! After the safety car retired again, Button slid up one spot and overtook two cars in the next lap and three in the following. By lap 51, Button had reached 10th position; he climbed to 7th position with 17 laps to go. Lap 54 saw him setting the fastest lap, and at the end of lap 64, the only cars in front of Button were driven by Michael Schumacher, Mark Webber, and Sebastian Vettel.

In the final lap, the only thing standing between Button and the checkered flag was Vettel, who, up until then, had driven a flawless race. Vettel's only mistake came toward the final chicane when he took a corner too wide, giving Button a chance to push past into first place and win the race.

Antony Hamilton didn't hold back and reminded Button that Vettel's mistake enabled the win. Others would say it was a combination of Button's incredible talent in harsh conditions along with his calm, calculated, and determined approach. If it hadn't been for his mental determination, he would never have gone from last to first with 6 pit stops in a race that lasted 4 hours and 39 seconds.

It was Button's greatest race and an extreme race for various reasons. To that date, it was the longest Formula 1 race, and it was the race that had the highest number of safety care deployments.[2] Funnily enough, Button also set the record for the slowest average race-winning speed at 46.518 miles per hour and was the world champion with the most pit stops and a win!

Button retired in 2016 after 18 seasons but is still involved in Formula 1. In particular, Button is pushing for more eco-friendly solutions, such as combustion engines that run on sustainable fuel to benefit the environment and bring back that awesome sound of the Formula 1 car.

16

THE RACE THAT NOBODY
WANTED TO WIN

" *"Anything can happen in Formula One...and it usually does."* [1]

— GRAEME MURRAY WALKER

The 80s was a strange decade for Formula 1. It began with the significant change to turbo engines. Renault had been struggling until 1977 when its advanced design came up with the first turbocharged engine. Essentially, engine exhaust gases are forced into the engine, giving cars a huge power boost. Generally speaking, a 1,500cc turbo engine was the equivalent of a 3,000cc normal engine.[2] By the 1982 Monaco Grand Prix, practically all cars were fitted with new turbo engines. This may have made sense on less challenging tracks, but we are talking about Monaco now!

Just weeks before, Formula 1 had lost another racing legend in the final qualifying session for the Belgium Grand Prix. Gilles Villeneuve (father of Jacques Villeneuve) went through the first chicane, but on the rise, he saw that Jochen Mass was traveling much slower. Mass moved to the right to let Villeneuve pass, but Villeneuve also moved to the right. Villeneuve's Ferrari hit Mass and flew into the air, landing 100 meters away. Villeneuve lost his helmet and was thrown another 50 meters on impact. He was taken off life support later that day.

The following race in Monaco was a cloudy and gray day, reflecting the mood after Ferrari's loss of Villeneuve. This left Ferrari with only one car in the Monaco Grand Prix, driven by Didier Pironi. René Arnoux, Riccardo Patrese, and Bruno Giacomelli had first, second, and third pole positions, respectively. Other drivers included Alan Prost, Keke Rosberg, Nigel Mansell, Niki Lauda, and Nelson Piquet. It should have been an interesting race!

Arnoux sped off to a good start and maintained his lead until the Swimming Pool section (named because of the pool next to the track rather than the conditions of the track). On lap 14, he hit a curb that caused his car to spin and crash. As he couldn't restart the engine, he was out!

After this, there was little drama, with a handful of cars retiring due to mechanical issues. In fact, it was such an average race that until lap 60, you could almost have said it was boring. With just a little rain, boring went to mayhem. The engines of the 1980s were notorious for oil drops. The oil and rain turned the track into something more like an ice rink. Pair that with the extra powerful engines, and you end up with the same number of cars retiring as finishing.

With 15 laps to go, Prost was in the lead with Patrese on his tail. Pironi was hanging in there despite driving without a front wing. As Prost managed to gain a bigger gap, the rain became heavier, but with the checkered flag so close, nobody was keen to head to the pits for a tire change. Eleven laps from the finish line, Roseberg hit a wall. This put Michele Alboreto closer in the lead, but his rear suspension failed with 7 laps to go; he was out. Derek Daly was also driving without a rear wing or a rear-view mirror, and his car was leaking a decent amount of oil, making it worse for the remaining eight cars.

Prost was still heading for a win until the last 3 laps. He came out of the chicane with the rear end spinning so much that he hit a barrier and shredded his wings and one wheel. He kissed goodbye to his first Monaco win, but Patrese was happy to be in the lead, especially after passing Prost's crash. His lead was to be short-lived, and on the final lap, he hit an oil spill, spun, and was left facing uphill. Because he was in a dangerous position, the marshals had to push him, and fortunately, he ended up facing downhill, so he could restart his engine. During this time, Pironi and Andrea de Casaris had passed him.

Pironi was almost not going to race because Ferrari thought it was disrespectful after Villeneuve's death. Pironi had finally decided to race and was probably glad he had until his car spluttered to a halt with no fuel. That should have put de Casaris in the lead, but the same thing had happened to him a few hundred meters before. Daly was next to crash one lap from the finish.

James Hunt, the 1976 world champion, was commentating on the race and summed up the final dramas well, "We've got a ridiculous situation where we're all sitting by the start-finish line waiting for a winner to come past, and we don't seem to be getting one!"[3]

BBC commentator Murray Walker described it as "Certainly the most eventful, exciting, momentous Grand Prix I have ever seen."[4]

With such a spectacle taking place, Patrese didn't even realize he was back in the lead, and because there was no radio communication, he wasn't even aware he had won his first Grand Prix.

The podium was just as interesting. There was talk of Patrese being disqualified because of the marshal's assistance, but moving him to safety had been necessary; it was just fortunate that he ended up in a position to jump-start his car. Next to him were Pironi and de Cesaris, despite neither of them actually seeing the checkered flag! Mansell managed to earn points after fighting back from 10th place to achieve 4th position.

He would go on to win five more Grand Prix with a total of 37 podium appearances. He retired in 1994, which, at the time, was Formula 2's longest career. Nevertheless, it wouldn't be the end of his racing days.

17

THE 13 CAR PILE UP

> "*I have to admit, it was a bit scary. I had no brakes, no steering, nothing was working. I was just sitting there hurtling down the track with wheels hitting me on the head and cars going all over the place.*"[1]

— EDDIE IRVINE

In 1998, drivers and teams headed to Spa to participate in the Belgian Grand Prix. It would be a race to remember and, for once, not because of tragedy (unless you count the financial loss!) Only eight cars would make it to the finish line, mainly because of one crash that involved 13 cars. In a crash that took 15 seconds, an estimated $13,000,000 in damages was caused![2]

The Spa circuit might not have the same fame as other challenging tracks, but it comes high on the list for many drivers, especially the Brits. British drivers have taken more than double the number of pole positions. At the other end of the scale, 68 drivers have a 0 percent finish rate.[3] The weather tends to make this track exceptionally challenging, but so do the bends. Each bend is epic as the track winds through the mountains. Drivers must also deal with Formula 1's steepest ascent through a corner and over a crest! Some of the 1998 drivers didn't even get that far!

The season was going well for Mika Häkkinen, driving for McLaren-Mercedes. He was leading with 77 points, and Michael Schumacher was just 7 points behind. Häkkinin's teammate, David Coulthard, was in 3rd place overall but a distance behind Schumacher. As there were only four races remaining in the season, it was mathematically impossible for any other driver to knock them off the first three positions. The Brits did well qualifying. Eddie Irvine, Schumacher's teammate, was 5th on the grid, and Damon Hill made a surprising appearance with 3rd place. Schumacher sat between the two Brits, and Coulthard and Häkkinen battled for first and second, with Häkkinen taking the prime spot by 0.163 seconds. But the conditions had been dry for the qualifiers, whereas race day was the complete opposite.

Like all the other drivers, Häkkinen, Coulthard, Hill, and Irvine had opted for full wet tires, and Jacques Villeneuve,

Jean Alesi, and Michael Schumacher had chosen their intermediate tires. As expected, Häkkinen made a good start with Villeneuve, Schumacher, and Giancarlo Fisichella behind. All cars made it around the first corner, but with so much spray on the road, visibility was horrendous. Coulthard dropped a wheel into a metal grille, which caused his car to spin across the track. What only looked like a bowling ball taking down its pins, car after car joined the pile up with wheels and debris flying from a mass of chaos and mist.

Amazingly, of the 11 teams that started, only one team escaped without damage to both cars. Ralf Schumacher and Damon Hill, driving for Jordan, were both behind Coulthard before the accident, but skillful driving and quick thinking allowed them to pass untouched. As per the rules at the time, a stoppage within the first two laps meant the race would have to start. Drivers involved in the crash started emerging from the scene, racing back to the pits for their spare cars, but it turned out not to be necessary. It took over an hour for the track to be cleared, and the race restarted with 4 fewer cars.

The race finally restarted, with Hill taking the lead, followed by Häkkinen and Michael Schumacher. But the first lap wiped out a few more cars! At the first corner, Häkkinen lost control, and Johnny Herbert crashed into him with his Sauber. Both drivers had to retire. On the same lap, Alex Wurz and Coulthard collided, forcing

Wutz to retire. The race was down to 15 cars before the end of the first lap.

By the 26th lap, seven more cars had retired, including Eddie Irvine, who spun his Ferrari off the track. Then, a rather heated retirement by Michael Schumacher grabbed people's attention. Schumacher had a 40-second lead on Hill and was about to overtake Coulthard. Despite being instructed to let Schumacher pass, he didn't do so immediately. Instead, the two came down the track. Coulthard slowed down to let Schumacher pass but didn't move from the racing lane. Because the conditions were so bad, Schumacher drove straight into the rear of Coulthard but amazingly drove back to the pits on three wheels. One lap later, the same thing happened to Giancarlo Fisichella and Shinji Nakano, with Fischella retiring.

Luck seemed to remain on team Jordan's side. With so many cars now retired, it was down to Hill and Ralf Schumacher. But it wasn't smooth sailing for Jordan team boss Eddie Jordon. Schumacher was in the process of suing Jordan to release him from his contract, and there was no guarantee that he would listen to team orders. After being told to hold back, Jordan watched in angst, hoping there wouldn't be a battle for first place. Schumacher did as instructed, securing Jordan with an amazing 1-2 finish. Michael Schumacher was less than pleased, and after a confrontation with Coulthard in the pits, he went on an angry rage, telling Jordan that his brother wouldn't race for him again and bought out his contract for $2 billion. All in all, it was an expensive race, to say the least!

18

WHEN DRIVERS REFUSED TO RACE

> "We have been watching Ferraris for fifty years. Ferrari has had God knows how many drivers. They come and go but still all that people want to see is a Ferrari. They cannot see the bleeding driver anyway! Really, I ask you, what asset are they?"[1]
>
> — BERNIE ECCLESTONE

It was once thought that when it came to performance, there was an 80-20 rule, which implied 80 percent of a race's success was down to the car and the team while only 20 percent of the success was thanks to the driver. This was probably the mindset of Ecclestone, former chief executive of the Formula One Group.

Research from 2012 to 2019 confirmed what drivers in the 80s already knew: Ecclestone was wrong. The success of a race is an intricate combination of the driver, the car, and the interaction between the driver and the car. It's more like 20 percent car influence and 15 percent driver influence, with their interactions having a 30 to 40 percent influence. The better the driver, the more they can get out of a car's technology. At the same time, drivers play a significant role in car development and racing strategy. Naturally, money has its part to play, too. Data collected from eight seasons showed that if a team wanted to move from 10th position to 9th, they would need to invest a whopping $164.6 million![2]

Ecclestone's extremely harsh words came during a Formula 1 strike, and instead of calming the tension, his words demonstrated why drivers would go on strike. Who wouldn't when the big boss speaks like that? So, what caused drivers to strike and for Ecclestone to respond in such a way?

After teams had spent most of their focus switching to turbo engines in 1980, the next two years saw significant changes. Niki Laude had returned just 3 years into his retirement thanks to McLaren's most lucrative offer in Formula 1 history at that time. Riccardo Patrese, who hadn't been successful, joined the Braham team with reigning world champion Nelson Piquet. Williams had won the constructor's championship and was now pleading with Alan Jones not to retire. In the end, he was forced to sign a rush deal with Keke Rosberg, who hadn't won a single point in the 1981 season.

Behind all of these changes, political tension was brewing. The first race of the season was to be held in South Africa, but trouble arose after FISA (Formula 1's governing body) had slipped in some new contract clauses, with many unaware of the changes. Niki Lauda had always been a stickler for details and driver well-being; he spotted the clauses and refused to sign.

One of the clauses stated that drivers would only be allowed to say positive things about FISA. The previous seasons had been nothing but turbulent, and making it illegal for drivers to criticize the governing body was ridiculous and unfair. What angered drivers more was the clause stating they couldn't negotiate contracts with teams themselves and only team bosses would do the negotiating. The first drivers to join Lauda were Didier Pironi, current GPDA (Grand Prix Driver's Association) President, and Gilles Villeneuve. Rene Arnox, Bruno Giacomelli, and Andrea de Cesaris were soon to follow.

On the Wednesday before the season's first race, the drivers' representatives met with the Formula 1 Commission. Pironi was clear that the drivers wouldn't race unless the clauses were changed, but FISA President Jean-Marie Balestre was not about to compromise. Despite other drivers signing the contract, Lauda and Pironi encouraged them to protest if no changes were made.

Things got even more serious on Thursday when drivers were supposed to participate in the practice sessions. The

GPDA had organized a minibus in the event that nothing had changed. The minibus planned to take the drivers to the Sunnyside Park Hotel, but race organizers decided to park their minivan at the track's exit so that the drivers couldn't leave. Perhaps this wasn't the best strategy to stop a group of some of the world's best drivers. Jacques Laffite, a French driver for the Ligier team, simply got off the GDPA minibus, got into the minivan, and moved it out of the way. Twenty-nine Formula 1 drivers made their way to the hotel. Only Jochen Mass was missing because he hadn't yet made it to the practice session.

Ecclestone, who was also the boss of Brabham at the time, claimed he had fired Piquet and Riccardo. The race would be postponed, and anyone participating in the strike would receive a lifetime ban from Formula 1. Ecclestone, obviously not one to mince his words, said that none of the drivers would be missed and were easily replaced.

Barricaded in a conference room in the hotel, drivers kept themselves entertained. Villeneuve began to please the crowd by playing on a piano but was seriously upstaged by Elio de Angelis and his talented concert-level Mozart renditions. Bruno Giacomelli drew cartoons and taught the other drivers how to dismantle an AK-47, thanks to his time in the military. Lauda became a stand-up comedian!

Not everyone was pleased to be there. The younger drivers seemed not to fully understand what was going on. Keke Rosberg didn't see the point in the strike but remained in support of the other drivers. Teo Fabi "ran like a chicken" and apparently escaped from a bathroom window, leaving Rosberg furious. [3] No other driver respected Fabi again, not because he left but because he went straight to Ecclestone and Balestre and passed on what the drivers had been discussing.

Some team members tried to get into the conference room to persuade their drivers, but the piano got its second use for the night and was used to block the doors. All the while, Pironi tried hard to negotiate, with little success.

It wasn't until Friday morning that there was a break. Mass was the only car on the track while he took part in some practice laps. As other teams had nothing better to do, they all held up boards with different lap times, and at one point, he was even black-flagged because of a blockage on the track. FISA and Balestre finally backed down but Ecclestone was still fuming and refused to let Piquet drive, claiming he hadn't slept during the ordeal. After passing a medical test, Piquet proved he was fit to drive.

Organizers agreed that the clauses would be dropped from the contracts, and Balestre assured the drivers there would be no repercussions for their strike. Although the clauses were dropped, various fines of between $5,000 and $10,000 were handed out along with some race bans, though the drivers got them reduced.

The drivers proved their worth in the qualifiers, with the first six pole positions all being cars with the newer turbo engines that had caused so many adjustments prior to the strike. Arnoux, Piquet, and Villeneuve took the first three spots, but it was Alain Prost who went from 4th pole position to winning the race and going on to win the championship. The strike had been a success not only for the amended contracts but also because the experience, especially a night locked in together, unified Formula 1 drivers, a crucial step forward after the rocky years they had had.

19

IS THERE A PLACE FOR WOMEN IN FORMULA ONE?

> *"I dared to be different, I want to inspire others to do the same."*[1]
>
> — SUSIE WOLFF

Since the first Grand Prix in 1950, there have been 775 Formula 1 drivers. Throughout these 1,093 races, there have been just five female drivers! There is no rule prohibiting women from competing, but considering the numbers, there certainly isn't a great deal of encouragement.

The lack of encouragement is just one issue. There are next to no role models for women keen on racing; despite being in the 21st century, equality is a huge problem. The fact is, if you had a male and female driver side-by-side with the same experience and talent, sponsorship would most likely go to the male driver. Although times are changing, female drivers must be seen and heard—starting with those who have paved the way for today's drivers.

THE COUNTESS DE FILIPPIS

Maria Teresa de Filippis, actually Countess de Filippis, was born in 1926. Her father was an automotive engineer, and her two brothers helped inspire her love for racing. At the age of 22, she entered her first race and went on to enter the minor Italian car championships. She was incredibly passionate and skilled and would have won the 1954 championship had it not been for a serious accident. The accident caused her to lose her hearing in her left ear.

In 1955, she returned to racing and secured a place on the Maserati team. Her debut Grand Prix appearance was in the 1958 Monaco race. She qualified 16th but couldn't participate in the race because of engine failure and missing parts. This same year, her boyfriend, Luigi Musso, died in the French Grand Prix.[2]

Her greatest Formula 1 success came in the Belgian Grand Prix, where she finished 10th. In 1959, de Filippis joined the Behra-Porsche team. Jean Behra was a friend of hers, and when he sadly died on the German track that same year, she decided to retire.

Nicknamed "the little pilot," de Filippis served as the president of the former Formula 1 drivers association in France and helped set up the Maserati Club.

LELLA LOMBARDI

Born in Italy in 1941, Lella Lombardi wasn't just the second female Formula 1 driver; she was also a gay Formula 1 driver. Today, this wouldn't be a shocker, but back in the days of the male-dominated industry, Lombardi broke the mold! She began in the Formula 850 races before moving to Formula 3 for 2 years, and in 1976, she was ready to make her Grand Prix debut but failed to qualify because of a driveshaft failure. In the 1975 Spanish Grand Prix, Lombardi became the first female to score Formula 1 points.

Lombardi had exceptional skill in handling what was considered a "real man's" car with its large 5.0-liter V8 motor. When the media asked how it felt to handle such big cars, she smartly replied, "I don't have to carry it, I just have to drive it."[3] Sadly, Lombardi died of breast cancer at the age of 50.

DIVINA GALICIA

Historically, the number 13 hasn't been used in racing because of two fatal accidents. The number has only been used twice, and considering the British are so superstitious, it is a surprise that Divina Galicia, Britain's first female driver, was the second person to race a number 13 car. Racing was a second career for Galicia after skiing. She competed in the Winter Olympics four times. Her racing career began with British Shell International Group in 1976, and in the same year, the team decided to enter her in the British Grand Prix but didn't qualify. Sadly, she didn't qualify for her two 1978 races either. Though she didn't score points in the World Championship, she made a podium appearance in the British Formula One Championship, and her greatest achievement was finishing 7th in her own M23.

DESIRÉ WILSON

Desiré Wilson is considered to be the woman who has achieved the most in racing. The South African has competed in CARTS, and she is the only licensed female to drive in a CART IndyCars event. She holds a FIA Super License, meaning she can race at the highest level.[4] She has competed in Formula 3, Formula 2, and the 24 Hours of Le Mans.

In 1975, Wilson became the first female to win a Formula Ford race in South Africa. She decided to move to the U.K. in 1980, where she entered the British Formula 1 Championship. That same year, racing for Brands Hatch, she earned the title of the first female to win any kind of Formula 1 race. Wilson retired in 1984 but continued as a coach and commentator. She is still a respected figure in the racing world, as she was entered into the South African Hall of Fame in 2019 for all she achieved in motor racing.

GIOVANNA AMATI

Giovanna Amati was born in 1959 into a very wealthy family, so much so that she was kidnapped in 1978 for 75 days and only returned after a ransom was paid that would be today's equivalent of more than $3,000,000. Some feel that Amati was promoted to Formula 1 before being fully prepared. She was only given the place because Braham couldn't sign another driver. Unfortunately, Amati didn't qualify for any of the three 1992 Formula 1 races, but she did go on to win the Women's European Championship the following year.

SUSIE WOLFF

Though not actually competing in a Formula 1 race, Susie Wolff deserves a mention. In 2014, Wolff became the first woman to roll out a Formula 1 car at a race weekend in 22 years. (The last time was when Amati failed to qualify.) She drove for Williams in the practice sessions at the German, Spanish, and British Grand Prix. In 2016, Wolff joined Mercedes as an ambassador and test driver. Two years later, she joined Venturi Racing as a shareholder and, the following year, became part of the powerhouse partnership of Mercedes and Venturi to form Mercedes EQ.

Wolff dedicates a lot of her career to encouraging women into the field. Today, she is the managing director of the F1 Academy. As of 2023, the F1 Academy is set to launch a new all-female driver category so that young female drivers have more support and opportunities to progress through W Series, Formula 3, and Formula 2. Drivers will have access to more track time and the chance to work with renowned professional teams to help them physically and mentally prepare. Though it might be a few more years before this talent is part of the norm, it's great to see a change coming.

20

THE EMERGENCY SERVICES THAT DID MORE HARM THAN GOOD

> *"You have to do everything possible for the safety of the competitors, spectators and the people who work in F1. But we mustn't emasculate it. But mustn't take away the spectacle."*[1]
>
> — DAMON HILL

When all the focus is on the world's fastest cars and drivers, it's easy to miss what goes on behind the scenes. The Formula 1 cars aren't the only wheels to hit the tracks. Safety cars and even the medical car have their own history.

SAFETY CARS

Safety cars are an essential part of Formula 1 protocol. Any incident requiring one of the marshals to intervene means the safety car will deploy, and drivers have to remain at a certain speed and distance from each other behind the safety car until the conditions are safe again.

The safety car first appeared in the 1973 Grand Prix in Canada. Bad weather meant the Porsche 914 made its debut appearance, but in some confusion, the car picked up the wrong lead driver. Most cars ended up a lap down with nobody sure of the winner for hours. The safety car made a few appearances in the 80s, but it wasn't until 1993 that it became an official fixture. Various cars were used for three seasons, but not every car, like the Fiat Tempre, could handle the pace. This is why, in 1996, Formula 1 and Mercedes entered a contract whereby Mercedes would be the sole provider of the safety car. It was only in 2021 that Mercedes brought in an Aston Martin Vantage as a second safety car. Since 2000, the safety car has been driven by Bernd Mayländer. Thanks to modern technology, there is even now a virtual safety car system. The VSC enables race officials to slow down the pace of the cars without deploying the actual safety car.

MEDICAL CARS

The medical car is a different story. The medical car was introduced in 1987 after the accident that took Ronald Peterson's life. At the time, Sid Watkins, the official Formula 1 doctor, insisted changes were made, including the medical car and a helicopter on site.

Not only does the safety car need to arrive at an accident in seconds, but it must also carry the medical equipment. The safety car is lightweight; the medical car can weigh up to 2 tons. The occupants of this car aren't paramedics. Instead, it's a certified FIA doctor, who, at the moment, is Dr. Ian Roberts.[2] In the driver's seat, there is Alan van der Merwe· Formula Ford Festival and British Formula 3 champion.[3]

The medical car is equipped with impressive technology. The team of two has a live feed and GPS tracking, and they receive data from the biometric gloves the drivers wear. The doctor can monitor oxygen in the blood, pulse, and hand movements. If there is an accident, the G-sensor informs the doctor of the impact of the crash so they are better prepared when they reach the accident. As well as the medical car, there are two R-cars (rescue cars) that can take one doctor and four paramedics to an accident. A medical professional can be at a scene anywhere on the circuit within 30 seconds.

IMPROVED SAFETY

Both the safety and medical cars need to be out on the tracks beginning Thursday before the race. Much like the Formula 1 cars, they need to ensure there are no mechanical issues, the tires are bedded, and nothing can go wrong.

At the scene of an accident, van de Merwe's role can change. Sometimes, he will give medics a hand; other times, he only needs to stay in the car and inform race control what is happening. There are occasions when he has had to direct ambulances and other recovery vehicles. Aside from the formation lap behind the competing cars, the hope is not to see the medical car!

Drivers may hate it more when the safety car is deployed. No reasonable human being would wish their competitors harm, but the safety car has its own problems. When the safety car is deployed, drivers aren't allowed to overtake and must reduce speed to a certain limit. This closes the gap between them, which is ideal if you are running last but not so much for the lead. During the time the car is on the track, tires begin to cool down, and this has an impact on the performance when the race starts again. This is why you will see drivers weave behind the safety car in the hope of keeping tires warmer.

Drivers often push Mayländer, and after so much experience, he can recognize a driver not by his car but by their strategy to insist he goes faster. Michael Schumacher would sit in Mayländer's blind spot. Lewis Hamilton brakes and accelerates. Max Verstappen is a Formula 1 pup compared to the seasoned Mayländer, but that didn't stop him from comparing the safety car to a turtle, even though race officials set the speed limits.

NOT SO SAFE

The overall consensus is that the safety car is needed until you ask the likes of Taki Inoue. Inoue freely admitted to being a pay driver (driving for free with personal sponsorship or funding) who wasn't good enough for Formula 1. He appeared in 18 races and didn't manage to score any points. In fact, he only managed to finish five of the races. But that's not what he is remembered for. In 1995, Inoue suffered a mechanical issue during the qualifiers at the Monaco Grand Prix. He was being pulled back to the pits when a safety car plowed into him, causing his car to flip. Fortunately, Inoue had remembered to put his helmet back on, and he walked away, still able to race the next day. Of the 26 cars that started the race, only 10 finished, with Inoue retiring on lap 27 because of his gearbox.

As if that wasn't enough, the same year, Inoue was in the Hungarian Grand Prix when his car caught on fire. Marshals rushed over with fire extinguishers but Inoue obviously didn't feel like their effort was enough. He walked a few paces to grab another extinguisher and as he turned to head back to his car, he was hit by the medical car! Inoue landed on his feet and was able to make a joke out of it later "Very good, perfect landing, I think nine-point-nine-nine", but the hit was hard enough to injure his leg and miss the next race.

Inoue decided that that would be his last season in Formula 1 and since the days of Mayländer and van de

Merwe, both the safety cars and medical cars are doing their jobs without bizarre mishaps!

21

THE LEAST SOUGHT-AFTER RECORD

"I always thought records were there to be broken."[1]

— MICHAEL SCHUMACHER

It's perfectly natural for drivers to rise up through the Formula 1 ranks, beginning their careers in karting before moving on to one of the tamer races. After all, you can't run before you can walk. It's common to see drivers excel in Formula 4, 3, and 2, but as soon as they reach Formula 1, their talent doesn't seem to meet the bar. This was the case for Indian driver Narain Karthikeyan. Before delving into how he achieved one of the least sought-after records, let's appreciate why drivers often struggle with transitioning to Formula 1!

MULTIPLE FORMULAS

Formula 4 is the youngest of the Formula Series races and was only introduced in 2014. There are no global races, but competitors get to build on their karting skills with regional races at top speeds of around 130 miles per hour.

One of the biggest differences between these races and Formula 1 is that they are all done in the same car. Mygale provides all Formula 3 cars, and Williams F1 designs Formula 2 cars. The reason all drivers use the same cars is that it's their individual talent that is seen rather than the focus being on a car's specific performance.

Power is another thing that varies. The Formula 3 cars have a top speed of around 167 miles per hour, and they don't have a Drag Reduction System (DRS),so the fun is seen around the corners. [2] A Formula 2 car may have top speeds of just 20 miles per hour less than a Formula 1, but the power is intensely different. The Formula 2 cars have a 500-horsepower engine and can hit 10,000 revs per minute. Sit in a Formula 1 car; the horsepower is around 1,000 and up to 18,000 revs per minute.

LE MANS

Another switch often seen is between the 24 Hours of Le Mans and Formula 1; however, the races couldn't be more different. Formula 1 is about intensity and speed over no more than two hours. Le Mans is a full 24 hours. Both require immense physical and mental skill, but being good at one doesn't automatically imply success in the other.

Only five drivers have managed to win the Formula 1 title and the 24 Hours of Le Mans. These include Mike Hawthorn, Jochen Rindt, Phil Hill, Graham Hill, and, more recently, Fernando Alonso. While many others have competed in both and won races, not all have made such triumphant transitions.

KARTHIKEYAN

Narain Karthikeyan was introduced to racing at a young age. His father won the South India Rally seven times, and this led the young Karthikeyan to have the ambition of becoming India's first Formula 1 driver. He began his professional racing career when he moved to the U.K. in 1994 and raced in the Formula Ford Zetec series. The same year, he entered the British Formula Ford Winter Series and became the Indian driver to win a European championship.

The following year, he entered four races in the Formula Asia Championship. In 1996, he won the Formula Asia International series, not only the first Indian to do so but also the first Asian. In 1997, he was back in the U.K. for the British Formula Opel Championship before his debut in British Formula 3 in 1998. In 2000, Karthikeyan took 4th place in the British Formula 3 Championship. On top of that, he has had three 24 Hours of Le Mans victories.

With all of these achievements, the next logical step was Formula 1, but after his debut in 2005, Karthikeyan was a way off from the podium despite scoring an interesting record.

In his 2005 season, Karthikeyan scored 5 points, which is better than some drivers new to Formula 1, but some years later, this Indian racing legend achieved something that no other driver had or has managed to do. He came in 24th!

This Formula 1 phenomenon is known as a full house. The number of cars that can start has changed throughout the years, but it is rare for all cars to actually start. When every starting car manages to finish, it's called a full house. So far, this has only ever happened six times in the history of Formula 1.

The first full house was in the Dutch Grand Prix when 15 cars started and finished. In 2005, the United States Grand Prix only saw 6 cars starting after 14 cars pulled out because of concerns with Michelin tires. That same year, all 20 cars that started in the Italian Grand Prix finished. In Japan, the 2015 and 2016 Grand Prix finished with full houses—20 and 22 starters, respectively.

The 2011 European Grand Prix started as one would expect. The race was held in Valencia, and Sebastian Vettel became the first driver to finish in the top three in the first eight races of the season. It was no surprise that Vettel secured pole position. Mark Webber, Lewis

Hamilton, and Fernando Alonso were on the grid behind him in that order. Timo Glock filled the final positions on the grid in the 21st spot and Jérôme d'Ambrosio in the 23rd pole position, both racing for Virgin-Cosworth. In the 22nd position, HRT-Cosworth had Vitantionio Liuzzi driving for them, and teammate Karthikeyan had the final 24th pole position. Cosworth was a new team then, and to match with the likes of Red Bull Racing-Renault, McLaren-Mercedes, and Ferrari would be a challenge.

Vettel took the checkered flag with Alonso coming in just over 10 seconds behind him. Soon to follow were Webber and Hamilton. The last leaving the grid looked similar to the first.

In retrospect, considering the age and experience of the Cosworth drivers and the rarity of every car finishing, the full house was still impressive. The two Virgin-Cosworth drivers finished 21st and 22nd. Liuzzi landed 23rd place, and Karthikeyan came in at what would normally be a disappointing last place. But this was the only race where 24 cars had started and 24 had finished. It might not be the ideal result, but Karthikeyan still made a childhood dream a reality when he competed in and finished a Formula 1 Grand Prix.

Finishing last in a Formula 1 race might not be the most desired record, but we can't overlook the bigger picture. One young boy had a dream to race with some of the greatest drivers in the world, and he achieved this dream.

For his nation, he gained a number of records, which earned him the Padma Shri award from the Indian Government, the fourth-highest award given to a civilian. In the world of Formula 1, his record might be the least sought, but for a nation, he inspired!

22

JUST HOW DANGEROUS IS FORMULA 1?

> *"The closer you are to death, the more alive you feel. But more powerful than fear itself, is the will to win."*[1]

— JAMES HUNT

It's possible that many of us can remember the old cars without seatbelts, which is shocking considering seatbelts were invented in 1959.[2] Nevertheless, there is a difference between our parents or grandparents getting from A to B and Formula 1 driving! It's hard to believe that seatbelts weren't compulsory in the early days of the series. Fortunately, the improved safety conditions have seen a dramatic reduction in the number of Formula 1 deaths.

In the 1950s, there were 15 deaths on Formula 1 week-ends.[3] The first death was in 1952 when British racer Cameron Earl crashed during a test race. Between 1953 and 1957, the tracks took the lives of Chet Miller, Charles de Tornaco, Onofre Marimón, Mario Alborghetti, Manny Ayulo, Bill Vukovich, Eugenio Castellotti, and Keith Andrews. The late 50s were horrendous for the Brits and Americans. British drivers killed included Peter Collins and Stuart Lewis-Evans, and Americans lost Pat O'Connor, Jerry Unser, and Bob Cortner. And, of course, there was the loss of racing legend Luigi Musso.

Gradually, these numbers began to fall, but it was a very slow process. In the 60s, 12 drivers were killed, and in the 80s, 4 drivers lost their lives. In the 90s, only 2 deaths occurred, but the fact that both occurred on the same weekend was enough to spark significant changes. In 1994, Ayrton Senna was the last Formula 1 death during a race until 2014, when Jules Bianchi failed to slow his car down and plowed into the back of a crane that was removing a damaged car from a previous accident. So, in the history of Formula 1, the 00s remains the only decade where the death of a driver wasn't seen.

Formula 1 is a sport of excitement and speed, and finding the balance between these elements and safety is challeng-ing. Is Formula 1 still a dangerous sport? Does the increased speed mean more danger, or do the safety measures create some sort of balance? Let's look at what changes have been made.

Probably the most extreme thing about Formula 1 safety is the fact that cork helmets were only introduced in 1952. The first two seasons allowed drivers to compete without medical backup or a safety net. In 1955, cars had switched from front-engines to mid-engines, and disc brakes were added.

By the 60s, stricter safety measures were implemented. Cars needed a roll bar installed at least 50mm above the driver's helmet in case the car flipped over. Flag signals were introduced, as were electronic system interrupters. Finally, in 1968, a full-visor helmet made it to the scene, worn by Dan Gurney. Fire safety greatly improved. A double fire extinguishing system began in 1969, and in the later years of the decade, fireproof suits were recommended, although these suits didn't become mandatory until 1971.

Watching drivers getting hurled from their cars, especially Jochen Rindt's accident in Monaca, led to the first six-point safety harness in 1972. At the time, he had been using four of the five points on the harness in case he needed to escape a fire. The impact of his crash was so hard that he slipped until the seatbelt slit his throat.

The 70s also saw headrests in cars and cockpit openings were increased to make it easier for a speedy exit. Some drivers began wearing the five-layer fireproof overalls; one in particular was Niki Lauda after he nearly died in a horrific fire.

Carbon fiber monocoques became standard in the 1980s. This material, still used today, is almost indestructible. Since then, the chassis of the cars have only continued to improve safety levels for the drivers. General Motors performed the first barrier crash test on its cars in 1934, but it wasn't until the 80s that crash testing Formula 1 cars became standard, and the official safety care crash test started in 1992.

Fortunately, safety measures were extended to other race officials in 1994 when all refueling crew members had to wear fireproof clothing. As technology grew, computer analysis was introduced to identify dangerous corners, and data recorders in cars were able to measure data after an accident. Wheels were tethered to the chassis to stop them from flying off in an accident, and in the 2000s, this became a double tether after flying tires killed two marshals.

In the last two decades, technology has generally enhanced the safety of Formula 1, especially since the introduction of the virtual safety car. Tire barriers were replaced with plastic blocks that absorb 40 percent more energy. In 2003, the HANS device was introduced to stabilize the head and neck in an accident, and in 2018, we saw the first HALO device.

The halo is a wishbone-shaped titanium bar at the top of the cockpit and wraps around the driver's head. The halo is designed to hold the weight of a London double-decker bus— that is the equivalent of 12 ton Surprisingly, many opposed the halo at first because of the looks. Formula 1 boss Bernie Ecclestone was slow to be persuaded, and Lewis Hamilton called it "the worst-looking modification" in the history of Formula 1.[4] He soon retracted that opinion when he crashed in the Italian Grand Prix, admitting that the halo had saved his life. And it has saved multiple lives since. It's widely believed that the halo would have saved Senna.

Many avid fans have pointed out how certain Formula 1 executives' opinions may have impeded safety progress. Ecclestone has, on more than one occasion, treated drivers like a commodity rather than human beings, and this was only confirmed when he favored car appearance over one of the greatest safety features Formula 1 has introduced.

By the 70s, cars were getting faster, but tracks weren't being improved to match the new speeds, and basic equipment and training were lacking. In the 1973 Dutch Grand Prix, Roger Williams got a puncture, spun into the barrier, and slid across the track in flames. David Purley stopped his car and attempted to flip Williams's car and save him. Marshalls who had fire extinguishers stood and watched. Two other marshals attempted to put out the fire but quickly gave up. The most the marshals did was stop the crowd from jumping on the track to help Purley flip the car. Williams died!

There is an unspoken hero in the world of Formula 1. He is a man who, over his 27 years in the industry, made crucial changes, not just in physical safety but mental health as well; he showed genuine care for the drivers. Professor Sid Watkins spent 4 years in the Royal Army Medical Corps before specializing in neurosurgery and joined Formula 1 as the safety and medical delegate in 1978.

That same year, Watkins was at the Italian Grand Prix and couldn't get to the track to save Ronnie Peterson. His legs were broken, and it took 20 minutes to get him to the medical center. Once there, Watkins stabilized Peterson and was then transferred to hospital, but complications led to Peterson's death. Watkins then made demands to Ecclestone, leading to massive changes in medical procedures. This included better safety equipment, an anesthetist, a medical car, and a medical helicopter at every race. This was a huge step forward because, at the time, medical attention was little more than a temporary tent.

At the time of Peterson's accident, Senna was one of the first on the scene. He had checked Peterson's breathing and stabilized his head. Thankfully, he had watched Watkins do the same in the past and was keen to learn. Watkins considered teaching all drivers breathing and head stabilizing techniques, something that was introduced in 1990.

Watkins retired in 2005 after receiving an Order of the British Empire and saving the lives of Nelson Piquet, Mika Hakkine, James Hunt, Ruben Carrichello, and many others with the changes he made. He was unable to save his close friend Senna, but this only spurred more changes. [5]

Watkins passed away in 2012, but his legacy lives on. Today, a full medical center is at every circuit and, although smaller, is equipped with the same as an emergency department. The 24-hour staffed center has a surgeon, an anesthetist, resuscitation equipment, and an operating theater. As well as paramedics and ambulances, there is a helicopter and an additional helicopter outside the circuit as a backup. A doctor, paramedics, and a pilot are on standby. If, for any reason, the helicopter can't land at a nearby hospital, the race won't go ahead. [6]

Going back to the question, "How dangerous is Formula 1?" Thanks to the likes of Sid Watkins, it is far less dangerous. Thanks to technology and engineering, drivers are far more protected than ever. Undoubtedly, there will be more accidents and probably deaths, but fortunately, death is not seen as part and parcel of racing or accepted as part of the glory!

BIZARRE FORMULA 1 RECORDS

"If everything seems under control, you're not driving fast enough." [1]

— MARIO ANDRETTI

I t's a race of speed, so it goes without saying that Formula 1 drivers strive for records, especially regarding the fastest lap. It's not just the driving that requires haste. Any unnecessary delay in the pits can steal the lead from even the best driver. In the 1950s, the average pit stop time was 67 seconds. The world record was set in 2023 with a jaw-dropping 1.82 seconds. [2]

This record was achieved by the Red Bull team—masters in the pit. The team is so skilled that in 2019, they performed a tire change in zero gravity! The Fastest Pit

Stop Award began in 2015. Ferrari won the most awards that year and Williams the following. Mercedes had a chance in 2017, but since then, Red Bull has snapped up the points. It might seem like it's just a fresh set of tires, but it takes exceptional organization and precision, and teams deserve recognition. These points go toward the World Constructor's Championship, for which Ferrari holds the record. Ferrari has taken home the Constructor's Championship 16 times!

Speaking of speed, Kevin Magnussen holds the record for the fastest speed in a qualifying session, hitting 218.5 miles per hour in 2022. In a Formula 1 race, Valtteri Bottas holds the record from 2016 when FIA officially clocked the speed at 231.4 miles per hour. Honda still holds the record for the fastest-ever speed in a Formula 1 car, however this wasn't in a race. While attempting to break the 400-kilometer-per-hour barrier, the driver made it 397.360 kilometers, the equivalent of 246.908 miles per hour. [3] The driver to achieve this in 2006 was none other than Alan van der Merwe, Formula 1's medical car driver.

As for the fastest overall race, this title goes to Michael Schumacher. In the 2003 Italian Grand Prix, Schumacher completed the race in 1 hour 14 minutes and 19.838 seconds. This gave Schumacher an average speed of 153.842 miles per hour. This is quite a difference when compared to Al Pease's slowest average speed of around

43 miles per hour when he was disqualified for driving too slowly.

No record is too bizarre for Formula 1. Luca Badoer entered 58 races between 1993 and 2010 and started 50 of them, but during his entire career, he didn't score a single point. He is considered the most skilled driver to never earn a World Championship point. That has to sting, but he isn't the only one. Dave Walker raced for Lotus in 1972 and did not score any points. However, his teammate, Emerson Fittipaldi, won the entire championship and, at the time, was the youngest driver to do so at just 25.

Sebastian Vettel is considered to be among the best of Formula 1 drivers. Between 2007 and 2022, Vettel started 299 races and made 122 podium appearances with a total of 3098 points. He won 4 World Championships consecutively from 2010 to 3013, one of his records. The first win made him the youngest at the time, aged 23. He also holds the record for most pole positions in a season, starting first 15 out of the 19 races. There is one record Vettel would probably rather forget—his debut appearance. After leaving the garage, Vettel accelerated in the pit lane and received a penalty, earning himself the record for the fastest penalty within 6 seconds of his career.

Formula 1 has a wide age range when it comes to competitors, more than most sports. Max Verstappen was the youngest driver to ever compete in a Grand Prix at 17 years and 166 days old. Then, 14 days later, he became the youngest driver to score points. The oldest driver to score points was Philippe Étancelin at 53 years old and 259 days in the 1950 Italian Grand Prix.

Because of improved safety in Formula 1, it's common to see a driver's career last for years. In the early days, only 11 drivers who began their careers in the 50s raced for more than a decade. Graham Hill was a rarity as he remains in the top 10 longest careers. Beginning in the 50s, Hill's career lasted 16 years, 8 months and 8 days. Michael Schumacher had the longest career of 21 years and 3 months until Fernando Alonso celebrated 22 years as a Formula 1 driver, and he isn't ready to retire just yet. On the other hand, the shortest career wasn't just a season or even a single race. Marco Apicella was racing in his home country of Italy. On the first corner of the first lap, there was a multi-car collision, and Apicella was forced to retire from the race. His Formula 1 career lasted 800 meters. Many consider Apicella to have the shortest career. This title belongs to Ernst Loof. In the 1953 Grand Prix, Loof, who was also racing in his home country, made it just 2 meters off the grid before his fuel pump failed.

If only there were awards for determination in Formula 1. Stirling Moss won 16 Grand Prix but never took a championship. Nico Hulkenberg started 179 races but never saw the podium. And the Arrows/Footwork team entered 382 races and never saw a win. Andrea de Cesaris holds the record for most starts without a win, entering 208 races, but Claudio Langes has the record for 14 qualifying attempts without even making the grid!

Over the previous 22 chapters, it is clear that to name one Formula 1 driver as the best is impossible. Lives have been cut short before drivers could reach their potential, tracks have changed, and cars have vastly improved. In the 1950s, Juan Manuel Fangio won 5 Championships and was runner-up twice in just 7 seasons. Imagine what he could have done in Max Verstappen's Red Bull RB19. There are too many factors to name the greatest driver. Nevertheless, there have definitely been remarkable achievements.

Fernando Alonso holds the record for the most races started, at 370, and he won the World Championship title twice. Lewis Hamilton has started 325 races and successfully took home the Championship seven times. Michael Schumacher also has 7 Championship titles, but he achieved this with just 306 starts! Hamilton has won 103 Grand Prix and Schumacher 91. On the other hand, Hamilton has had 104 pole positions and Schumacher just 68. Schumacher maintained his champion title for an astonishing 1,813 days until a young Alonso took it from him in 2005.

The debate of the greatest driver won't be settled anytime soon, but this final bizarre record will be hard to beat. In the 1996 Monaco Grand Prix, 85.7 percent of cars retired.

In a rather unusual race, all three drivers to finish made it onto the podium, including Olivier Panis, David Coulthard, and Jonny Herbert. Before this, no other driver had won at Monaco after having started behind the 8th car on the grid. Panis started 14th on the grid.

24

THE EMOTIONS BEHIND RACING

> *"You will never know the feeling of a driver when winning a race. The helmet hides feelings that cannot be understood."[1]*

— AYRTON SENNA

To many, Formula 1 appears to be a hard boys club where feelings are left behind, and there is only room for velocity and rivalry. This chapter will prove that, despite the image, there have been numerous moments of extreme emotions in Formula 1.

THE LOWS

Ayrton Senna's death has been mentioned on more than one occasion for good reason. It wasn't a sorrow that one driver suffered. It wasn't even an incident that one team mourned. Every member of Formula 1 felt the loss, and so did the nation. Brazil was suffering from poor growth, hyperinflation, and political turmoil, and the year before had seen three notorious massacres that caused major human rights issues. Brazil turned to their racing hero to escape the events of daily life.

There was no doubt that Senna had created a list of rivals over the years. Alain Prost is obvious, but Eddie Irvine, Damon Hill, and Nigel Mansell were others. Mansell saw that Senna could "intimidate pretty much every driver on the grid."[2] He was part of the old-school drivers where respect was earned. This would have been particularly hard for the likes of Schumacher, who burst onto the Formula 1 scene and became serious competition for Senna. By 1994, things had calmed down, and the two had developed a respect for each other but the rivalry wasn't over. This season was especially tense for Senna and Schumacher; it was showdown time! Schumacher had won the first two races, but Senna was in the lead at Imola when he had his fatal accident.

Though it was the 90s, there was still much less information compared with today. At the time, Schumacher assumed that Senna would be okay; perhaps he'd miss a few races but nothing worse. Senna's death, combined with the death of Ronald Ratzenberger, caused intense feelings for Schumacher, so much so that he doubted his future in Formula 1. He didn't attend Senna's funeral because he went test driving to try and make a future about his career and also because he didn't want to mourn in public.

The extreme display of emotions came several years later, in 2000. Schumacher had won the Monza Grand Prix and his 41st victory. At the post-race press conference, Schumacher was asked what it felt like to tie Senna's record. Schumacher bowed his head and began to cry. This was completely out of character for Schumacher and has not been seen since, but it just goes to show that though some drivers are gone, they are not forgotten.

A more recent death hit one Formula 1 driver harder than expected, and the crowd showed immense support. It was 2019, and the Formula Series was back after a long summer break. The good spirits didn't last as Anthoine Hubert, Juan Manuel Correa, and Giuliano Alesi had a bad crash during a Formula 2 race. Hubert and Correa's cars were torn apart. Correa fractured both legs and suffered a minor spinal injury. Hubert didn't make it.

Hubert was just 22 when he passed away, and this was a shocker for his childhood friend, Charles Leclerc. The two had grown up karting before joining Formula teams. Not only this, but Hubert's death was the first since Leclerc's godfather, Jules Bianchi. On that Sunday's race, just 24 hours after his friend's death, Leclerc passed the scene of Hubert's accident on the formation lap, obviously numb and hurt. On the 19th lap (Hubert's racing number), the crowd gave Leclerc a standing ovation. Leclerc went on to win the race and his first Grand Prix, which he dedicated to Hubert.

Speaking of Bianchi, the Formula 1 community and drivers both paid an emotional tribute to the driver. The number 17 car was retired as a mark of respect to the late 25-year-old. Bianchi passed away nine months after crashing into a crane that was recovering another car during 2014 Japanese Grand Prix. Fifteen minutes before the 2015 Grand Prix in Hungry, 20 drivers placed their helmets on the tarmac, with Bianchi's in the center, and huddled around them. Along with Bianchi's family, they stood in a minute's silence.

THE HIGHS

At the other end of the emotional scale, there are the victories. Every victory will be a thrill for the driver and the team, but some stand out more than others. In the final moments of a race, the suspense is intense—especially for the drivers. For Felipe Massa, the burning suspense lasted a whole 39 seconds in 2008.

It was the season's final Grand Prix, and the Ferrari driver needed Lewis Hamilton to come in 6th or worse for Massa to secure the Championship title. Massa's pole position served him well as he beat Fernando Alonso, Kimi Räikkonen, and Sebastian Vettel. Hamilton wasn't having the best race and was even behind various non-title contenders. The Ferrari team was jumping for joy for a whole 39 seconds before Hamilton passed Timo Flock, making it to 5th position. Poor Massa kissed his Championship goodbye.

When Lewis Hamilton beat Michael Schumacher's 91-win record, over the moon doesn't quite cut it. But behind the scenes, one person was overcome with emotions. Hamilton's father, Antony, hugged his son and marveled at the dedication his son had shown. Back in 1993, the family had nothing when Hamilton wanted to start karting.

Nigel Mansell's first victory was epic, deserving, and heartfelt by many. The man had suffered from a broken neck, second-degree burns, and 5 years of trying. The crowd went mad in true "Mansellmania" style. The man could barely stand, and as the British Anthem played, Mansell looked as if he still couldn't believe that he was on the podium. The most emotional wins would go to Sebastian Vettel after his first Championship in 2010 and Ruben Barrichello's first win at the 2000 German Grand Prix. Neither driver could hold back the tears, a testimony of how hard they worked to achieve these titles. Another worthy emotional victory came from Kimi Raikkonen in the 2018 US Grand Prix after winning his first race in more than 5 years. The response from the usually laid-back driver showed just how much this sport meant to him.

Perhaps the moments that affect us the most are those when rivals come together to show support, respect, and admiration. When Vettel retired, Lewis Hamilton posted, "Seb, it's been an honor to call you a competitor and an even greater honor to call you my friend. Leaving this sport better than you found it is always the goal."[3]

One of Formula 1's most iconic retirement images goes to Felipe Massa. Massa was racing in his home country of Brazil. In his final race before retirement, Massa crashed into a barrier near the start-finish straight. The only thing to do was walk back to the pits with the Brazilian flag wrapped around his shoulders with his other hand wiping away the tears. The crowd of thousands cheered him on, and an emotional yet supportive team and family met him!

25

COULD THIS BE ONE OF THE GREATEST RACES OF ALL TIME?

> *"Everyone wants to see racing. This is what F1 is for and this is what it is."*[1]
>
> — JOS VERSTAPPEN

Statistics, wins, and titles can help identify the greatest drivers, but what makes the greatest race? Some people would consider the overtakes and the constant battles for the lead. For them, the Dutch Grand Prix of 2023 would have thrilled them with a record-breaking 186 passes. This is the opposite extreme of the 2003 Monaco Grand Prix, the 2005 US Grand Prix, and the 2009 European Grand Prix, with absolutely zero overtakes.

For others, it's the sheer unpredictability and the uncertainty, the interesting race strategies, and though few would admit it, the odd minor crash does increase the tension. Racing heroes and legendary car constructors complete the ingredients for a great race. Out of the hundreds of Grand Prix races over the decades, a few tick all the boxes. One in particular was the 1993 European Grand Prix!

It was the 29th European Grand Prix held at Donington Park. As one would predict, the weather was more than typical of Britain, wet and dismal. The torrential rain led to a crowd of only 50,000. To add to the challenging conditions, it was very cold! The third race of the World Championship saw Alain Prost returning after a year out and Michael Schumacher and Ayrton Senna were ready for their next battle. So far, Prost had won the opening race of the season, but Senna arrived at Donington ahead in the championship points.

Prost had secured the pole position driving for Williams, and Williams was in a great position with a 1-2 qualifying with teammate Damon Hill in second position on the grid. Schumacher was third on the grid in his Benetton-Ford, and the dry weather on Saturday left Senna in his McLaren behind Schumacher. In a twist of irony, Senna's debut in Formula 1 was on the same track but for Williams 10 years before. Other worthy mentions are Riccardo Patrese, Schumacher's teammate in 10th place, Jonny Herbert who was in the 11th spot driving for Lotus, and Rubens Barrichello behind Herbert. Only Luca Badoer failed to qualify with the 25 cars on the grid. At the time, there was no such thing as intermediates, so each of the 25 cars had their full-wets on.

Juan Manuel Fangio, John Watson, and Fernando Alonso have had some spectacular laps during their careers. All of these could be classed as the greatest laps, but none have been good enough to be called the "Lap of the Gods," which occurred on Donington's first lap.

The green light appeared, and the Williams superior cars made an excellent start. Schumacher's Benetton was the latest version without traction control. So, his start was particularly impressive but not as remarkable as Karl Wendlinger in his Sauber. Senna was not convinced about the underpowered Ford V8 engines. This had caused some controversy off the track. Senna had only agreed to drive on a race-by-race basis and was trying to get a spot on the William's team, but Prost insisted on a contract that prohibited Senna from joining the team. Senna may not have gotten off to the best start, but his skills would make up for any doubts about the engine.

As the drivers approached the first corner, Redgate, Schumacher squeezed Senna and enabled Karl Wendlinger to push Senna back to 5th position, and soon after, Wendlinger passed Schumacher. [2], By the Craner Curves, Senna was having none of it and passed Schumacher coming up alongside Wendlinger by the next bend known as Old Hairpin. Passing him, Senna's next challenge was Hill. He used the inside of the McLean's bend to slip past Hill. Senna was in 2nd position, and the only car ahead was Prost's. The Melbourne Hairpin allowed Senna to give the crowd a spectator's dream as he slid into the lead with confidence and exceptional timing, hitting the brakes on the penultimate corner. It wasn't just that Senna passed his competitors; he did so in one lap with an inferior car!

By lap 20, Senna had a 5-second advantage, and Prost and Hill were keeping on each other's toes. There was a threat of sunshine, and cars raced to the pits for a change of tires. Senna thrived as the rain started pelting down. But there was plenty of drama still going on behind the contenders. In the first 30 laps, 10 cars had retired. Karl Wendlinger and Senna's teammate Michael Andretti collided on the first lap. The suspension of Gerhard Berger's Ferrari failed, and even Schumacher spun off the track on lap 22. Four more cars would retire before lap 70.

Senna dominated the race. Hill managed to gain the lead during one of Senna's pit stops, but it was short-lived. In the end, Prost stopped in the pits 7 times, and Hill visited the pits 6 times. Senna's confidence in the rain meant only 4 pit stops and one of those, he aborted, achieving the fastest lap of 1:18.029 minutes. By the time he took the checked flag, he had lapped everyone except Hill. Hill came in second and Prost third. As for Patrese, who began 10th on the grid, he finished 5th, and better than that, Herbert, who started 12th, finished 4th! Drama and tension throughout the entire race enabled Fabrizio Barbazza to earn a point in the 6th position after starting on the grid in the 20th position.

Sega had sponsored the European 1993 Grand Prix, so as Senna took to the podium, he was handed a Sonic the Hedgehog trophy, which was later replaced with the real trophy. Still, the Sonic trophy, a clever marketing ploy, is now on display at the McLaren Technology Center.

In the 1993 season, only four drivers won the Grand Prix races. Schumacher won the Portugal Grand Prix, while Hill won three consecutive races in Hungry, Belgium, and Italy. As well as the European Grand Prix, Senna won in Brazil, Monaco, Japan, and Australia. This wasn't enough against Prost's seven wins and earning the World Championship title.

The Constructor Championship went to Williams with 168 points and McLaren behind with exactly half the points. With first place and third place, Prost and Hill contributed to the points. For McLaren, Hakkinen contributed with his 4 points and Andretti with his 7 points. Senna finished 2nd in the season, boosting the McLaren team with his 73 points.

It was an extraordinary season with what will unarguably be one of the greatest races in Formula 1 history. What comes ahead is as unpredictable as the start of any race, but with a bit of luck, Formula 1 fans will continue to be blessed with races such as the European 1993 Grand Prix.

CONCLUSION

I have all the respect in the world for the young and older drivers who are breaking records and taking Formula 1 to all-new extremes today. Each time Formula 1 teams and drivers break the mold and go beyond the ordinary, it inspires the next generation to do the same. Soon, we'll see a whole new set of extreme races, including stories where women are also setting the pace. Self-driving Formula 1 cars are now being tested, with the possibility of a new racing league in the coming years.

Nevertheless, through my research into the most extreme races in Formula 1, there is one thing that holds my attention and admiration. It's the drivers of the 50s, 60s, and even 70s. Those who risked their lives—not because they were suicidal or wanted to die—but because it was an unfortunate part of racing. They pushed their cars to the limit on tracks that nobody would be allowed to race on today. And it wasn't for the money. Drivers would have won a fraction of what is paid out today. It was a different time, one that shouldn't be forgotten as each generation passes on the racing baton.

Formula 1 can teach us about grit and determination; it can inspire us when setbacks get in our way. It can show us that even the fastest drivers in the world can have a soft and sentimental side. Regardless of your age or background, these stories can teach us lessons that reflect our daily lives, and I hope you have discovered an extreme story that will keep you motivated on your own track in life!

 "I think the best track in the world is to be honest."[1]

— SEBASTIAN VETTEL

THE SPEED, THE PASSION, THE
TRAGEDY, THE VICTORY, THE
TENSION— FORMULA 1 HAS A LITTLE
BIT OF EVERYTHING FOR EVERYONE!

I genuinely hope that you have found inspiration in the 25 extreme stories of Formula 1. For me, it is a sport that is far more than just fast cars racing around a track and if I could ask one small favor, it would be to share your reviews on Amazon so that others can discover the rich history and future of Formula 1!

LEAVE A REVIEW!

Thanks a million and I look forward to meeting again in our next adventures in the series of extreme sports!

Scan the QR code for a quick review!

NOTES

INTRODUCTION

1. F1 Experiences, "10 Iconic Quotes from the History of Formula 1", January 21, 2021
   https://f1experiences.com/blog/10-iconic-quotes-from-history-of-formula-1

1. THE GREATEST DRIVER NEVER TO WIN FORMULA 1 WORLD CHAMPIONSHIP

1. Quote Fancy, "Top 15 Stirling Moss Quotes", 2023
   https://quotefancy.com/stirling-moss-quotes
2. Henry Kelsall, "Sir Stirling Moss Was The Greatest Driver Never to Win The World Championship", June 29, 2021
   https://www.hotcars.com/sir-stirling-moss-was-the-greatest-driver-never-to-win-the-world-championship/

2. THE TRAGIC END TO WHAT WOULD BECOME LEGENDARY

1. Quote Fancy, Top 4 Bruce McLaren Quotes, n.d.
   https://quotefancy.com/bruce-mclaren-quotes
2. Kiowa County Press, "Interesting Facts About McLaren Automobiles, n.d.
   https://www.espn.co.uk/f1/story/_/id/24471861/sixty-years-ago-sportsmanship-cost-stirling-moss-world-championship
3. McLaren, "Bruce's Death: Courage in the Face of Adversity, June 2, 2023 https://www.mclaren.com/racing/heritage/bruce-mclarens-

death-courage-in-the-face-of-adversity-27789266/

3. THE FIRST GRAND PRIX TO LIGHT UP THE NIGHT SKY

1. Wikipedia, "2008 Singapore Grand Prix", September 29, 2023 https://en.wikipedia.org/wiki/2008_Singapore_Grand_Prix
2. Anirban Aly Mandal, "Why Is The Singapore GP Also Called the F1 Night Race?", September 9 2022 https://www.essentiallysports. com/f1-news-why-is-the-singapore-gp-also-called-the-f1-night-race/
3. James Phillips, "A Conspiracy Revealed: The 2008 Singapore GP", April 10, 2022 https://www.formulanerds.com/features/a-conspir acy-revealed-the-2008-singapore-gp/

4. THE MCLAREN RIVALRY THE WORLD LOVED TO WATCH

1. AZ Quotes, Formula 1 Quotes, n.d. https://www.azquotes.com/quotes/topics/formula-1.html
2. Thomas Maher, "Alain Prost Reflects: Ayrton Senna 'Lost His Bearings After I Retired'", January 21, 2023 https://uk.news.yahoo. com/alain-prost-reflects-ayrton-senna-170900596.html? guccounter=1#:

5. WHEN TIRES LEAVE A RACE A DRIVER OR TWO SHORT

1. GrandPrix Race Hub, "Sunday Team Quotes, June 19, 2005 https://www.grandprix.com/races/united-states-gp-2005-sunday-team-quotes.html
2. Williams F1, "All You Need to Know About F1 Tyres in 2023", March 28, 2023 https://www.williamsf1.com/posts/faf938a0-

663c-4ccc-b76b-199433864f6b/everything-you-need-to-know-about-f1-tyres-in-2023

3. Adam Cooper, "The 2005 US GP Farce: The Full Inside Story, June 19, 2020 https://www.motorsport.com/f1/news/the-2005-us-gp-farce-the-full-inside-story/4809048/

6. EVERY MILLISECOND COUNTS

1. Quote Fancy, "F1 teams need a driver who will consistently set lap times that are 100 percent on the edge.", n.d.
   https://quotefancy.com/quote/1547896/Jean-Alesi-F1-teams-need-a-driver-who-will-consistently-set-lap-times-that-are-100

2. Filip Cleeren, "Top 10: The Closest Finishes in Formula 1 History", April 13, 2021, All times are taken from here.
   https://www.motorsport.com/f1/news/top-ten-close-finishes-f1/4778094/#gal-4778094-m0-michael-schumacher-ferrari-rubens-barrichello-ferrari-11794774

7. A SERIES OF UNFORTUNATE EVENTS THAT COST A TITLE

1. James Phillips, "A Conspiracy Revealed: The 2008 Singapore GP", April 10, 2022 https://www.formulanerds.com/features/a-conspiracy-revealed-the-2008-singapore-gp/

8. FORMULA 1'S GREAT COMEBACK

1. Pinterest, "Inspirational Quotes by Niki Lauda", n. d.
   https://www.pinterest.com/pin/films-qoutess-3--573364596281930644/

2. "Jo Siffert Dies in Crash, YouTube, July 9, 2023. https://www.youtube.com/watch?v=MRudd44Iggg&pp=ygUKam8gc2lmZmVydA%3D%3D

3. Gerald Donaldson, "Nigel Mansell", July 2, 2015
   http://www.f1speedwriter.com/2015/07/nigel-mansell.html

4. "Niki Lauda Full Episode, YouTube, September 10, 2013.
   https://www.youtube.com/watch?v=u7nS0EHm7sI
5. Scuderia Fans, "Arturo Merzario Recalls Saving Niki Lauda's Life", n.d.
   https://scuderiafans.com/video-former-ferrari-driver-arturo-merzario-recalls-saving-niki-laudas-life-after-horror-crash/
6. Mercedes AMG, "Niki Lauda Friend", n.d.
   https://www.mercedesamgf1.com/team/person/niki-lauda

9. TRAGEDY ON THE TRACK

1. AZ Quotes, "Ayrton Senna Quotes", n. d.
   https://www.azquotes.com/author/13321-Ayrton_Senna
2. Raphael Orlove, "Just How Horrifying Was the Worst Crash in Motorsports, Le Mans '55?", June 14, 2014.
   https://jalopnik.com/just-how-horrifying-was-the-worst-crash-in-motorsports-1589382023
3. Somin Bhattacharjee, "Queen of Rock 'n' Roll" Tina Turner Once Awed Ayrton Senna with an Emotional Tribute on Stage", May 25, 2023
   https://thesportsrush.com/f1-news-queen-of-rock-n-roll-tina-turner-once-awed-ayrton-senna-with-an-emotional-tribute-on-stage/

10. FATHER AND SON RACING

1. Reuters, "Motor Racing-Rosberg Sees Genetics as a Big Part of F1 Success", March 11, 2017.
   https://www.eurosport.com/formula-1/motor-racing-rosberg-sees-genetics-as-a-big-part-of-f1-success_sto6397263/story.shtml
2. Andrew Lewin, "Ex-F1 Champ Nelson Piquet Heavily Fined for Racist, Homophobic Slurs", March 25, 2023
   https://f1i.com/news/469821-ex-f1-champ-nelson-piquet-fined-for-racist-homophobic-slurs.html

11. POLE POSITION MIGHT NOT BE EVERYTHING

1. Paul Fearnley, "Teo Fabi: "He Didn't Need a Kiss or a Cuddle", n.d.
   https://www.motorsportmagazine.com/archive/article/may-2012/98/a-kiss-and/
2. Louis Pretorius, "How Important Is Pole Position in F1?", November 29, 2021.
   https://onestopracing.com/how-important-is-pole-position-in-f1/
3. Paul Fearnley, "Teo Fabi: "He Didn't Need a Kiss and a Cuddle".", n.d.
   https://www.motorsportmagazine.com/archive/article/may-2012/98/a-kiss-and/

12. FROM THE CLOSEST FINISH TO THE GRAND PRIX THAT LEFT EVERYONE WAITING

1. Formula1, "Jim Clark- What Made Him So Good?", April 21, 2018
   https://www.formula1.com/en/latest/article.jim-clark-what-made-him-so-good.6DXkoAanL2yMIyYE8AsauQ.html
2. Motorsport, "Top 5: Biggest Winning Margins in F1 History", n.d. All times taken from here.
   https://www.motorsport.com/f1/news/top-5-winning-margins-history/4788077/
3. Ziv Knoll, "Jim Clark, With a Splash", July 29, 2023
   https://humansideofracing.com/events/jimclark-spa-1963/

HOW MANY TIMES HAVE YOU BEEN SURPRISED BY THE EXTREMES OF FORMULA 1 SO FAR?

1. Gracious Quotes, "48 Niki Lauda Quotes: Quotes on Live and Racing (F1)", July 13, 2022.
   https://graciousquotes.com/niki-lauda/

13. WHAT TO DO WHEN YOU DON'T QUALIFY?

1. Team-BHP, "F1: Some Inspirational Quotes to Make Your Day", March 17, 2016
   https://www.team-bhp.com/forum/intl-motorsport/174216-f1-some-inspirational-quotes-make-your-day.html
2. Tom Leach and Dieter Rencken, "FIA Take Hard Stance on Porpoising: Or Be Disqualified", June 16, 2022.
   https://racingnews365.com/fia-take-hard-stance-on-porpoising-fix-or-be-disqualified

14. DETERMINATION AT ITS BEST

1. Pinterest, "F1 Quotes", n.d.
   https://www.pinterest.ca/F1SocialPress/f1-quotes/
2. Reuters, "Motor Racing-Rosberg Sees Genetics as a Big Part of F1 Success", March 11, 2017.
   https://www.eurosport.com/formula-1/motor-racing-rosberg-sees-genetics-as-a-big-part-of-f1-success_sto6397263/story.shtml

15. BUTTON'S ABILITY TO FACE THE MENTAL CHALLENGES OF FORMULA 1

1. Quote Fancy, "The fast, flowing parts, the high-speed corners, that's where a Formula One care is at its best- changes of direction, pulling high G-forces left and right.", n.d.
   https://quotefancy.com/quote/1116446/Jenson-Button-The-fast-flowing-parts-the-high-speed-corners-that-s-where-a-Formula-One
2. Reuters, "Formula One Statistics for the Canadian Grand Prix", June 14, 2023.
   https://www.reuters.com/sports/soccer/formula-one-statistics-canadian-grand-prix-2023-06-14/#:

16. THE RACE THAT NOBODY WANTED TO WIN

1. Autosport, "F1 Quotes that Influence You", November 5, 2008
   https://forums.autosport.com/topic/105092-f1-quotes-that-influence-you/
2. Jarrod Partridge, "The Golden Era of Turbos In Formula 1", January 20, 2021.
   https://f1chronicle.com/the-golden-era-of-turbos-in-formula-1-f1-history/
3. Luke Smith, "F1 Monaco GP 1982 Retrospective: Remembering F1's Craziest Finish", May 6, 2020.
   https://www.autosport.com/f1/news/f1-monaco-gp-1982-retrospective-remembering-f1s-craziest-finish-4982779/4982779/#:
4. Steven Pye, "Remembering the Tragedy and Mayhem of the 1982 F1 World Championship", October 14, 2013
   https://www.theguardian.com/sport/that-1980s-sports-blog/2013/oct/14/remembering-1982-f1-world-championship

17. THE 13 CAR PILE UP

1. Formula 1, "Do You Remember...the Massive Belgian Grand Prix Pile-Up", August 17, 2015
   https://www.formula1.com/en/latest/features/2015/8/do-you-remember_-the-massive-belgian-grand-prix-pile-up.html
2. Louis Pretorious, "How Expensive Is an F1 Crash?", December, 2021.
   https://onestopracing.com/how-expensive-is-an-f1-crash/
3. Nicky Haldenby, "Circuit de Spa-Francorchamps in Numbers", August 23, 2021.
   https://motorsportguides.com/circuit-de-spa-francorchamps-in-numbers/

18. WHEN DRIVERS REFUSED TO RACE

1. Keith Collantine, "1982 South African Grand Prix Flashback", June 18, 2008.
   https://www.racefans.net/2008/06/18/f1-drivers-to-strike-at-the-british-grand-prix-well-it-happened-in-1982/
2. Rachael Funnell, "Is Formula 1 Racing Success Down to The Driver, Their Team, Or Their Car?", July 7, 2022.
   https://www.iflscience.com/is-formula-1-racing-success-down-to-the-driver-their-team-or-their-car-64326
3. Dan Thorn, "That Time When the F1 Grid Went on Strike and Locked Themselves In a Hotel", February 7, 2020.
   https://wtf1.com/post/that-time-when-the-f1-grid-went-on-strike-and-locked-themselves-in-a-hotel/

19. IS THERE A PLACE FOR WOMEN IN FORMULA ONE?

1. Brainy Quote, "Susie Wolff Quotes", n.d.
   https://www.brainyquote.com/authors/susie-wolff-quotes
2. Scuderia Fans, "Luigi Musso's Life Story", n.d.

https://scuderiafans.com/luigi-mussos-life-story/
3. David Tremayne, "Trailblazing Racer Lella Lombardi Remembered, 30 Years on From Her Death", March 3, 2022.
https://www.formula1.com/en/latest/article.trailblazing-racer-lella-lombardi-remembered-30-years-on-from-her-death.6zz9pupcxc97yy5SEL1kkR.html
4. Mike Seymour, "The Beginner's Guide to…The Formula 1 Super Licence", February 8, 2023.
https://www.formula1.com/en/latest/article.the-beginners-guide-to-the-formula-1-super-licence.17Nai BXjs0O6SWZUIXrv9U.html#:

20. THE EMERGENCY SERVICES THAT DID MORE HARM THAN GOOD

1. Quote Tab, "Damon Hill Quotes", n.d.
https://www.quotetab.com/quote/by-damon-hill/you-have-to-do-everything-possible-for-the-safety-of-the-competitors-spectators
2. Andrew Benson, " Formula 1 Appoints Dr Ian Roberts as Medical Rescue Co-Ordinator", January 17, 2013.
https://www.bbc.com/sport/formula1/21070418
3. Mike Seymour, "The Beginner's Guide to…The Formula 1 Super Licence", February 8, 2023.
https://www.formula1.com/en/latest/article.the-beginners-guide-to-the-formula-1-super-licence.17Nai BXjs0O6SWZUIXrv9U.html#:

21. THE LEAST SOUGHT-AFTER RECORD

1. Brainy Quote, Michael Schumacher Quotes, n.d.
https://www.brainyquote.com/authors/michael-schumacher-quotes
2. Katie Osborne and Christian Hewgill, "F1 Explains: How DRS Works, Why It Was Introduced and What Is the Best Way to Use

It", September 1, 2023.
https://www.formula1.com/en/latest/article.f1-explains-how-
drs-works-why-it-was-introduced-and-what-is-the-best-way-to.
6Pfv07lvZNfTvqrXpxgVV7.html

22. JUST HOW DANGEROUS IS FORMULA 1?

1. Team-BHP, "Some Awesome Quotes from Legendary Drivers.",
   n.d.
   https://www.team-bhp.com/forum/intl-motorsport/174216-
   f1-some-inspirational-quotes-make-your-day-print.html
2. Volvo, "The Three-Point Seat Belt-An Innovation That Saved Over
   1 Million Lives, "July 15, 2019. Technically, the first seat belt was
   invented in the late 1800s.
   https://www.volvobuses.com/en/news/2019/jul/the-three-
   point-seat-belt-an-innovation-that-saved-over-1-million-
   lives.html
3. F1 Fandom, "List of Fatal Accidents", n.d. The number of deaths is
   based on Formula 1. There have been many more in motor racing
   overall.
   https://f1.fandom.com/wiki/List_of_fatal_accidents
4. Mihai Andrei, "The Halo Safety System in Formula 1 Was Hated
   by Fans and Drivers. It's Now Saving Lives.", July 4, 2022
   https://www.zmescience.com/science/halo-formula-1-
   04072022/
5. Andrew Benson, "Sid Watkins: F1 Safety and Medical Pioneer Dies
   Aged 84", September 13, 2012
   https://www.bbc.com/sport/motorsport/19578977#:
6. Christine, "F1 Safety- Medical Facilities", July 4, 2009.
   https://sidepodcast.com/post/f1-safety-medical-facilities

23. BIZARRE FORMULA 1 RECORDS

1. Team-BHP, "Some Awesome Quotes from Legendary Drivers, n.d.
    https://www.team-bhp.com/forum/intl-motorsport/174216-
    f1-some-inspirational-quotes-make-your-day-print.html
2. Formula 1, "Red Bull Smash Pit Stop World Record 2019 Brazilian
    Grand Prix", YouTube, November 18, 2019
    https://www.youtube.com/watch?v=BI75uWxEajA
3. Formula 1, "The Long Read: Chasing 400km/h In the World's
    Fastest F1 Car", November 3, 2017.
    https://www.formula1.com/en/latest/article.the-long-read-
    chasing-400km-h-in-the-worlds-fastest-f1-car.
    4KJFHbfjaU8GgqUEgsKQeU.html

24. THE EMOTIONS BEHIND RACING

1. Twitter, "Ayrton Senna Tribute", February 19, 2023
    https://twitter.com/F1_AyrtonSenna/status/
    1627096553885409282
2. Lawrence Barretto, "Ayrton Senna: Nigel Mansell Leads Tributes
    to 'Thoroughbred Racer'", April 30, 2014
    https://www.bbc.com/sport/formula1/27204026
3. Katy Fairman, "F1 Reacts to Sebastian Vettel's Emotional Retire-
    ment Announcement", 28 July, 2022.
    https://wtf1.com/post/f1-reacts-to-sebastian-vettels-
    emotional-retirement-announcement/

25. COULD THIS BE ONE OF THE GREATEST RACES OF ALL TIME?

1. Brainy Quote. "F1 Quotes", n.d.
    https://www.brainyquote.com/topics/f1-quotes
2. One 2 One, "Circuit Notes: Donington Park GP", n.d.
    https://www.one2one.uk.net/race-circuit-notes/donington-
    park-gp/

CONCLUSION

1. ESPN, "Sports Quotes", October 6, 2013.
   http://en.espn.co.uk/redbull/motorsport/quote/index.html?
   object=442

Made in United States
North Haven, CT
09 June 2024

53419466R00114